# TV
# LAND

# TV
# LAND

## A Guide to America's Television Shrines, Sets, and Sites

# ROBIN KEATS

St. Martin's Griffin
New York

*Design by Diane Stevenson SNAP-HAUS GRAPHICS*
*Maps ©1995 by Jaye Zimet*

*Title page credits:* Photo of Barbara Eden as Jeannie on page ii courtesy of Screen Gems. Photo of Don Adams as Maxwell Smart on page iii courtesy of Republic Pictures.
*Cover credits:* Postcard courtesy of The High/Widmeyer Archive. Photos *(clockwise),* from: *The Dick Van Dyke Show* courtesy CBS-TV; *Mork and Mindy* courtesy ABC-TV; *The Brady Bunch* courtesy ABC-TV; *Get Smart* courtesy Republic Pictures; *The Lone Ranger* courtesy the Wrather Corp.; *Lost in Space* courtesy 20th Century-Fox; *I Dream of Jeannie* courtesy Screen Gems; and *The Jetsons* courtesy Universal TV.

Library of Congress Cataloging-in-Publication Data

Keats, Robin.
    TV land: a guide to America's television  shrines, sets, and sites
/ Robin Keats
      p.  cm.
    ISBN 0-312-13194-1
    1. Television programs—United States—Miscellanea. 2. Imaginary places.
3. Television program locations—United States.
    PN 1992.3.U5K37   1995
    791.45'75'0973—dc20
                                               95-9894
                                               CIP

First St. Martin's Griffin Edition: July 1995

10  9  8  7  6  5  4  3  2  1

This book is dedicated to

**LAURA KEATS**

*who I met, married, and mated with*

*in*

**TV LAND**

*as well as in all other*

*parallel worlds*

*within reach*

# ACKNOWLEDGMENTS

The author wishes to thank Dr. Sheldon Benjamin, Jared Brady, Irene Brafstein, Susan Cane, Bonnie Eichenberg, Bonnie Fishelman, Jim Fitzgerald, Evie Greenbaum, Victoria Hugo, Sandra Kaplan, Ruth Keats, Jay Leno, Mark Lisson, Mara Lurie, Diane Mancher, Whit Mather, Amy Mogland, Melinda Mullin, Cass Paley, and Jaye Zimet for their support and encouragement.

# CONTENTS

# CONTENTS

# CONTENTS

*The Brady Bunch.* This blended family of quintessential suburbanites found life in L.A.'s San Fernando Valley to be *groovy* during their early years in TV Land. Later on, they found their lifestyle to be *copacetic*.
*Courtesy of ABC-TV.*

# PREFACE

## Ever been to Mineral City?

Mineral City. That's where Roy Rogers used to go whenever he had something to do in town. If Roy ever needed to check the stagecoach schedule, he didn't have to ride his horse, Trigger, to the town's depot in order to find out. All Roy had to do was pick up the telephone and call. They'd tell him quick as anything. If there was ever any trouble in town (and when wasn't there any?), Roy would come riding in on Trigger, with his six-guns blazing away at the bad guys. Roy also had backup transportation: a horseless carriage (a Jeep called "Nellybelle") that he kept parked back at his Double R Ranch.

Cowboys, cars, telephones, and stagecoaches . . . that was Mineral City, a Wild West town where altruism and audacious anachronism easily coexisted.

The most perplexing of all things having to do with Mineral City, though, is: Where was it? How can such a place be found? Given the impossibility of locating a paradox, who's to trust that the town of Evening Shade, Arkansas, actually exists, or that Metropolis is nothing but a mirage marked on some mythical map, or that Walton's Mountain is nothing more that the height of whimsy? In fact, unlike Mineral City, all three of these places are real.

The poet Gertrude Stein never watched television, yet she once wrote, *"There is no there, there."* While she was only referring to the city of Oakland, California, one might easily argue that the same can be said of TV Land. After all, that's where Mineral City is . . . isn't it? What there really is in TV Land are multiple measures of truth as well as massive measures of make-believe; a little of each add up to a new reality. Consider, for example, the two principal ways of getting to TV Land:

> If By Land: Take the *Highway to Heaven* out of *Hell Town*, go over *Falcon Crest* to *Melrose Place*; then north on *Flamingo Road* to *The Big Valley*; a left at *77 Sunset Strip* through *The Streets of San Francisco* to *The Outer Limits* and then ask *Gomer Pyle, U.S.M.C.,* or *The Fugitive* for directions to anywhere you want to go.

> If By See: Just turn the page and read on.

# INTRODUCTION

Since TV screens began to flicker with the light of electronic broadcasts, there've been approximately 5,000 different series that have been aired and watched by millions of viewers. Watching television is considered to be the number-one activity Americans really look forward to doing each day. According to one conservative estimate, we've already watched our screens for a cumulative total of over 224,372,599,000 hours!

Most of these hours were spent watching the many shows that took place in real locations, many that took place in very-much imagined locations, and a lot that took place in locations that were reality-based but reborn in fantasy. Together, all these places constitute the realm of TV Land: a world of time zones that differ not just in hours but often in decades, or in centuries, or in some cases even in millennia.

TV Land stretches from coast to coast, over oceans and across continents. It penetrates into the Earth and extends into outer space. The mythical and much-meandering path through it can be said to begin in prehistoric Bedrock and, after winding past such classic outposts of TV civilization as the Little House on the Prairie, the Ponderosa, and Mayberry, it reaches places beyond even the galactic frontiers of the Romulan and Klingon empires.

TV Land is intended to take you on several journeys along these paths—down to the depths of the Bat Cave and up to the summits of Twin Peaks, from the desert dunes of Death Valley to the subtropical shores of China Beach.

The book is divided into regional sections (Eastern, Southern,

Central, the Wild West, Western, and Far-Flung TV Land). Each of these sections begins with information intended to provide an overall perspective to each particular region: Every section includes an entry (or entries) that targets specific state, city, or other regional subcategory. All sections, likewise, contain a *Geographia* entry that deals with obscure facts and/or often overlooked lore, plus provides brief descriptions and the locations of real TV Land museums and historic sites.

# REALLY GOING TO. . . TV LAND

Following the above description, in regional progression, section by section, are detailed descriptions of the TV Land towns, shrines, cities, stores, and other sites that can actually be visited. The scope of TV Land is extensive, but it is not intended to include everything that's ever been seen or created on TV. The shows discussed herein were chosen because they're especially representational of their time, of their place, and of their significance in the history of television.

• • •

The Total TV Land section concludes the book with a treatment of topics that have to do with the whole of TV Land. The subject matter here, while mostly mythical, includes those elements that any great civilization must boast: transportation systems, military bases, prisons, hotels, restaurants, live-entertainment venues, vacation spots, health services, schools, media outlets . . . plus soap opera towns, pro sport teams, and a list of paranormals one might happen to meet along the way.

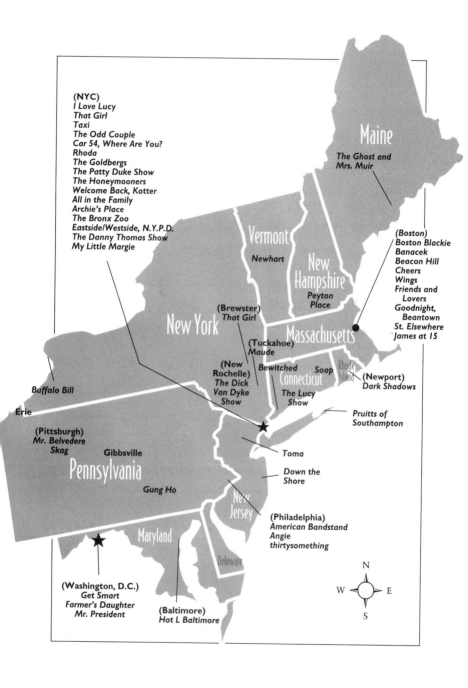

(NYC)
I Love Lucy
That Girl
Taxi
The Odd Couple
Car 54, Where Are You?
Rhoda
The Goldbergs
The Patty Duke Show
The Honeymooners
Welcome Back, Kotter
All in the Family
Archie's Place
The Bronx Zoo
Eastside/Westside, N.Y.P.D.
The Danny Thomas Show
My Little Margie

Maine

The Ghost and
Mrs. Muir

Vermont

Newhart

New
Hampshire

Peyton
Place

New York

(Brewster)
That Girl

(Tuckahoe)
Maude

(New
Rochelle)
The Dick
Van Dyke
Show

Bewitched

Connecticut

Soap

The Lucy
Show

Massachusetts

(Boston)
Boston Blackie
Banacek
Beacon Hill
Cheers
Wings
Friends and
   Lovers
Goodnight,
   Beantown
St. Elsewhere
James at 15

Rhode
Island

(Newport)
Dark Shadows

Buffalo Bill

Erie

(Pittsburgh)
Mr. Belvedere
Skag

Gibbsville

Gung Ho

Pennsylvania

Pruitts of
Southampton

Toma

Down the
Shore

New
Jersey

(Philadelphia)
American Bandstand
Angie
thirtysomething

Maryland

Delaware

(Washington, D.C.)
Get Smart
Farmer's Daughter
Mr. President

(Baltimore)
Hot L Baltimore

N

W        E

S

# EASTERN TV LAND

There are no plantation masters, no prairie-crossing pioneers, no bikinied damsels looking for shade beneath palm trees, and no cranky prospectors panning for gold in Eastern TV Land. There's been neither a cowboy nor a soldier nor an invading infidel from Mars who has ever set foot here.

It's this region's ethnic composition that distinguishes it from all of the other sections of TV Land. There are many nationalities and several forms of human life (including a vampire, a ghost, a witch, a pair of identical cousins, and even three employed television writers) thriving in the big cities, suburbs, and quaint villages of this region. Its phone book is filled with such names as Banacek and Bunker, Gravas and Goldberg, Montefusco and Muldoon, Kotter and Kojak, Skagsa and Stevens—names that bespeak many cultures. The East is where the Cuban Ricky Ricardo found it socially acceptable to marry the Scottish-American Lucy McGillicuddy. It's where a genuine birth certificate was issued to a future Sweathog named Juan Epstein.

Beginning in Maine, which is as east as one can get, a mythical tour would begin with a visit to the vampire, the ghosts, and a couple of writers (one real; one imaginary) who inhabit the state. The vampire, Barnabas Collins, is the 200-year-old inhabitant of Collins House in Collinsport and the central character of the gothic daytime serial *Dark Shadows*. The series' exteriors were shot, however, in Newport, Rhode Island. *Dark Shadows* ran from 1966 to 1971, and featured Kate Jackson long before she became one of Charlie's Angels.

Along the Maine coast are the mythical towns of Schooner Bay and Cabot Cove. Schooner Bay was where Edward Mulhare and Hope Lange, in the guise of *The Ghost and Mrs. Muir* (1968–69), shared Gull Cottage. Cabot Cove is the hometown of mystery writer Jessica Fletcher, played by Angela Lansbury in *Murder, She Wrote* (1984–). The real,

St. Elsewhere was the easier-to-say nickname of St. Eligius Hospital, which viewers were told was located in Boston. There is no St. Eligius Hospital in Boston, or elsewhere, but there is a Boston City Hospital. It's facade doubled for the TV Land institution's in which Dr. Robert Caldwell (Mark Harmon) and City Health Services Adviser Joan Halloran (Nancy Stafford) toiled and obviously kept in touch with each other. *Courtesy of NBC-TV.*

born-in-the-state-of-Maine writer, Grace Metalious, wrote a best-selling novel about the secrets and scandals of life in a New England town. The book was called *Peyton Place*. A movie version followed. And then, with the television program, *Peyton Place* became the most popular town in TV Land from 1964 until 1969. The first successful prime-time soap opera, it was telecast twice a week during its first season, three times a week during its second season, and then twice weekly, again, for the duration of its run. Its huge cast included Ryan O'Neal, Mia Farrow, Dorothy Malone, Dan Duryea, Mariette Hartley, Gena Rowlands, Ruby Dee, and Joyce Jillson, who later became a celebrity astrologer.

New Hampshire has never held much appeal for those who create TV shows. The make-believe town of Renfrew did, however, appear on TV screens from the fall of 1954 until the spring of 1955 as the setting for a show, *Willy*, about a lady lawyer. The title role was played by June Havoc. Small-town life apparently caused her to feel stifled and the series was reset by having her move to New York City.

Neighboring Vermont has been about as sleepy a place as New Hampshire. Its one well-known TV Land citizen, Dick Loudon (aka Bob Newhart), moved to the make-believe town of Norwich, Vermont, from Chicago, where his name had been Bob Hartley and where he had practiced psychology. Loudon bought and operated the Stratford Inn (said to have been built in 1774) from the fall of 1982 through the summer of 1990. The inn as seen on TV is actually the very real Waybury Inn, located in the town of East Middlebury, which is where *Newhart* filmed its exterior shots.

Connecticut has been an overwhelmingly popular state in terms of TV show settings. Samantha Stevens (Elizabeth Montgomery) exercised her magical nose in *Bewitched* (1964–72) while in residence at 1164 Morning Glory Circle in Westport.

The same town was also the setting for *My World and Welcome to It* (1969–72), which was based on the works of humorist James

Thurber. *The Lucy Show* (Lucille Ball sans Desi Arnaz) was set in Danfield from 1962 to 1968. *Soap* (1977–81), which starred Katherine Helmond, Billy Crystal, and Richard Mulligan, among others, took place in Dunn's River. Katherine Helmond remained in Connecticut when starring, along with Judith Light and Tony Danza, in *Who's the Boss?* (1984–92). *The Montefuscos* were also citizens of the Nutmeg State, albeit only for one month in the autumn of 1985.

New Jersey, the most densely populated state in the nation, has a high casualty rate when it comes to TV show locations. Although the *Miss America Pageant*, broadcast live from Atlantic City's Convention Center, goes on year after year, other series set in the gambling town by the sea have been very short-lived. *Big Shamus, Little Shamus*, in which Brian Dennehy starred as the house detective of the Hotel Ansonia, lasted for two episodes in the fall of 1979 and was the lowest rated series on television. *No Soap Radio* (with Steve Guttenberg, Stuart Pankin, and Bill Dana) was set at the Hotel Pelican. It lasted between the middle of April and the middle of May 1982. *Joe and Sons*, with Richard Castellano and Jerry Stiller, ran for five months during the 1975–76 season. It was set in Hoboken. *Dream Street*, from the creators of *thirtysomething*, was also set in Hoboken and ran for one month in the spring of 1989.

The longest lasting series ever to bear a New Jersey background was *Toma*. Based on the exploits of David Toma, an undercover Newark cop, it debuted in October 1973 and went off the air in September of the following year. *Toma* starred Tony Musante and Susan Strasberg. The real Toma made several guest appearances in disguise.

# NEW YORK CITY

## Manhattan

### Amos 'n' Andy

*Amos 'n' Andy* is the TV show responsible for Harlem becoming part of TV Land. The characters of Amos Jones, Andy Brown, Kingfish and Sapphire Stevens, Algonquin J. Calhoun, and Lightnin' all lived in the neighborhood around Lenox Avenue and 135th Street. Amos was played by Alvin Childress; Andy by Spencer Williams.

Based on a popular radio series created in 1925 by Freeman Gosden and Charles Correl (both of whom were white), *Amos 'n' Andy* came to television in June of 1951 and continued to produce original episodes through June of 1953. Not only was it the first TV show with an all-black cast, it was the only one able to make such a claim until *Sanford and Son* was aired in 1971.

*Amos 'n' Andy* was canceled after its seventy-eighth episode had been produced. The NAACP judged it to be racist and influenced the show's sponsor to withdraw its backing. Nevertheless, *Amos 'n' Andy* went on to become a huge hit in rerun syndication, playing in 218 American TV markets plus Guam, Austria, England, Bermuda, Nigeria, and Kenya. The rising strength of the civil rights movement, however, gave further impetus to totally extinguishing the lights in the Harlem of TV Land when, in 1964, the

Urban League called for the show to be removed from programming schedules. CBS, which owned the show, pulled it from syndication in 1966 and it has not been seen since.

One particular episode, which dealt with geography, illustrates how the series portrayed the black man as ignorant and easily duped. In it, Kingfish takes Andy on a trip to "see America in a trailer" and charges him $400 for the guided tour he conducts. The whole journey is conducted within Manhattan's Central Park. Kingfish describes North Dakota, for example, as "a fisherman's parasite," and upon reaching the area he's designated as that state, Amos finds a sign reading "North Dakota—The State to Unlax In." Kingfish has also put up other signs, such as "Welcome to Kentucky" and "Welcome to Wyoming—Danger—No Trespassing—Indian Uprising."

Amos is taken to the Central Park Zoo "to see the mountain lions." Sapphire and her mother happen by the two of them in the park and Andy asks them, "What are you two doing in Wyoming?" Their answer foils Kingfish's charade and spoils the trip for the innocent and absurdly stupid Amos: No wonder the show has been judged as demeaning.

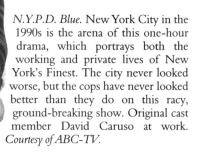

*N.Y.P.D. Blue.* New York City in the 1990s is the arena of this one-hour drama, which portrays both the working and private lives of New York's Finest. The city never looked worse, but the cops have never looked better than they do on this racy, ground-breaking show. Original cast member David Caruso at work. *Courtesy of ABC-TV.*

## Make Room for Daddy/The Danny Thomas Show

During the series' eleven years (1954–64), Danny Williams (played by Danny Thomas) and his family lived in Apt. 803 at 505 East 56th Street. As a professional comedian, Danny was on the road a lot and didn't get home as often as other fathers. When he did, he was treated almost as if he were a guest; hence the title of the show—which was subsequently changed to *The Danny Thomas Show* in 1958.

Eastern and Southern TV Land were linked together in one particularly memorable show in this series. It depicted Danny driving through the town of Mayberry, where he runs a stop sign and gets in trouble with the mayor, Andy Taylor. Though Andy was reassigned to the role of sheriff, this episode served as the pilot for *The Andy Griffith Show*.

## I Love Lucy

Lucy and Desi Ricardo (Lucille Ball and Desi Arnaz) lived in Apt. 4-A at 623 East 68th Street. This street number indicates that their apartment building must have been somewhere beneath the waters of the East River. Their pals, Fred and Ethel Mertz (Bill Frawley and Vivian Vance), were their landlords. During the course of the show—from October of 1951 through June of 1957—the Ricardos and Mertzes traveled to Europe, Florida, Cuba, and California, and shared a country home in Connecticut.

## That Girl

Born and raised in Brewster, New York, Anne Marie (played by Danny Thomas's daughter, Marlo) moved to the big city. Her new address was 344 West 78th Street, Apt. 4-D. She later moved down and across town to 627 East 54th Street. It didn't matter. Donald (her boyfriend, played by Ted Bessell) could always find her during the series' run from 1966 to 1971.

## Taxi

The Sunshine Taxi Company was at the corner of Hudson and Charles streets in Greenwich Village from the fall of 1978 through July of 1983. The Dover Garage, whose exteriors can be seen on TV, occupies the site. Danny DeVito, Judd Hirsch, Marilu Henner, and Tony Danza were in the cast.

*"Be it ever so humble, there's no place like hell (the garage)."*

—Alex

## The Odd Couple

This series (1970–75) was based on the Neil Simon play about sportswriter Oscar Madison (Jack Klugman) and photographer Felix Unger (Tony Randall), who share Oscar's apartment at 1049 Park Avenue. There's an apartment building with this number, but there's no apartment 1102.

# Subterranean Manhattan

## The Man from U.N.C.L.E.

The acronym "U.N.C.L.E." stands for the United Network Command for Law Enforcement. The program ran from September of 1964 to January of 1968. Agents Napoleon Solo (Robert Vaughn) and Ilya Kuryakin (David McCallum) reported at its headquarters, which occupied a second-level sub-basement complex beneath the streets of Manhattan. Its entrance was disguised as Del Florio Tailor's Shop, and was said to be somewhere in the East Forties. There have been reports that visitors to the United Nations, confusing the UN with U.N.C.L.E., have requested tours of the UN building's second-level basement in the belief it was the real site of Solo and company's activities.

## Beauty and the Beast

Underground Manhattan was also the setting for this series (1988–90) in which a pack of misfits—the deformed, disfigured, disregarded, and otherwise disenfranchised—found refuge from society beneath the city's streets. Lead by a poetry-quoting, lion-faced man named Vincent, they made their homes in subway tunnels, subterranean power stations, equipment vaults, and other underground sites. Ron Perlman played the Beast; Linda Hamilton was the Beauty.

# The Bronx

## The Goldbergs

The Goldbergs (1949–51) are TV Land's oldest sitcom family. They lived at 1038 East Tremont Avenue in the Bronx. This parcel of real estate is, therefore, one of the oldest deeded properties in the annals of TV history.

# Car 54, Where Are You?

The Bronx lit up on TV screens again when the 53rd Precinct opened up its doors in the fall of 1961. It was twelve years after the Goldbergs first put the Bronx on the TV Land map. Like the Goldberg home, the 53rd Precinct was also on Tremont Avenue. The show's interior scenes were shot in the Bronx at the old Biograph Studios on West 175th Street. City Island, which is nearby, was where exterior footage was usually shot. This series was the first cop sitcom. It starred Nipsey Russell, Joe E. Ross, and Fred Gwynne (the future Herman Munster). Car 54 was permanently parked in the fall of 1963.

> *"There's a holdup in the Bronx/Brooklyn's broken out in fights/Car 54, where are you?"*   —theme song lyrics

# Rhoda

It's not hard to imagine Rhoda Morgenstern (Valerie Harper) growing up in the Goldbergs' neighborhood, being that Rhoda is akin to being a member of "The Goldberg Family: The Next Generation." Rhoda's wit, insecurity, and warmth reflected the Bronx culture to millions of fans who, born too late to know the Goldbergs, might have otherwise missed out on the comedy of this urban corner of TV Land. Rhoda Morgenstern probably paid more moving bills than anyone else in TV Land, and it wasn't as if she lived all over, either. She just moved back and forth, down a couple of floors, or around the corner. According to TV travel records, she left her childhood home, at 3517 The Grand Concourse, at the age of twenty-four. Resettling in the Midwest of *The Mary Tyler Moore Show*, Rhoda rented an apartment on Waverly Street in Minneapolis.

She returned to the Bronx on September 9, 1974, and moved

back in with her parents. But her stay was not for long. She split for Manhattan and moved into her sister Brenda's Greenwich Village apartment. Her marriage to Joe Gerard, who had a ten-year-old son from another marriage, prompted yet another relocation, to another apartment in the same building. Rhoda's final move was to a smaller apartment, at 332 West 46th Street, after her divorce. *Rhoda* ran from the fall of 1974 until the end of 1978.

> *"I was born in the Bronx, New York, in December of 1941. Eventually I ran to Minneapolis, where it's cold and I figured I'd keep better."* —Rhoda

# Brooklyn

## Welcome Back, Kotter

Gabe Kotter (played by Gabe Kaplan) educated a class of slow learners, of semi-illiterates in other words, nicknamed the Sweathogs, at James Buchanan High School in Brooklyn. Had Ralph and Alice Kramden seen fit to bring a child into the TV Land world, he or she might well have attended this school in Bensonhurst that was supposedly filled with underachievers. Teacher Gabe and his wife (Marcia Strassman) lived at 711 East Ocean Parkway. They later moved to 1962 Linden Boulevard. Among Kotter's Sweathog students was Vinnie Barbarino, the role that launched the career of John Travolta, who later starred in the quintessential movie about life in Brooklyn, *Saturday Night Fever*, and recently starred as a bloated hero in the movie *Pulp Fiction*.

The Kramdens and the Nortons dwelled in working-class Brooklyn, across the East River from the Ricardos and Mertzes who could afford Manhattan's high cost of living.
*Courtesy of CBS-TV.*

*"As we say in the sewer, if you're not prepared to go all the way, don't put your boots on in the first place."*

—Ed Norton

## The Honeymooners

Jackie Gleason was born and raised in Brooklyn. Ralph Kramden, played by Jackie Gleason, lived there, too. Ralph and Alice (portrayed by Audrey Meadows) lived very modestly at 728 Chauncey Street in the Bensonhurst section. There are some who dispute this address and claim that the right number is 328. Others insist that the Kramdens lived at 358 Chauncey Street, which was Gleason's real boyhood address . . . but Gleason grew up in the Bushwick, not Bensonhurst, section! What is absolutely certain, however, is that Ralph spent his work day driving Gotham Bus Company's #247 on its Madison Avenue run. Ed and Trixie Norton (Art Carney and Joyce Randolph) were the Kramdens' best friends and their upstairs neighbors in whatever Chauncey Street apartment building they all lived in.

# The Patty Duke Show

Patty and her identical cousin Cathy (who hailed from Scotland) lived at 8 Remsen Drive in Brooklyn Heights and attended Brooklyn Heights High School. When the series debuted in 1963, Patty Duke, at the tender age of nineteen, became the youngest person ever to have a prime-time show bearing the name of its star. Pop stars Frankie Avalon, Chad and Jeremy, and Bobby Vinton all were guests on this series, which ran through the end of August 1966.

Patty Duke played identical cousins named Patty and Cathy Lane. Patty was an all-American girl; Cathy was very, very British and a guest in Patty's home. They both attended the fictitious Brooklyn Heights High School for the three years (1963–66) that the series lasted.
*Courtesy of ABC-TV.*

# Queens

## All in the Family

Archie and Edith Bunker (Carroll O'Connor and Jean Stapleton) lived at 704 Houser Street in the Corona section of Queens. They lived there with their daughter, Gloria (Sally Struthers), and son-in-law, Mike "Meathead" Stivic (Rob Reiner). This series, which ran from January of 1971 through the third week of September 1983, is considered one of the most important in TV Land history. Bunker, a dock foreman at the Prendergast Tool and Die Company, was a through and through, white working-class bigot. His Queens blue-collar neighborhood was populated by minorities with whom he was forced to coexist. His next-door neighbors, *The Jeffersons*, were black. His son-in-law was Polish. The Lorenzos, other neighbors, were Italian. When Archie was temporarily laid-off from his job, the Bunkers took in a Puerto Rican boarder to help with the rent. In 1977, Archie bought Kelsey's Bar and (at the end of that TV season) Gloria, Meathead, and their little boy, Joey, moved to California. During the 1979–80 season Archie took on a Jewish partner, played by Martin Balsam, to expand the bar business with a short-order restaurant. After Edith's death, which was dealt with in the first episode of the 1980–81

*Right:* Sally Rogers (Rose Marie), a TV comedy writer in her late twenties, lived and worked in New York City and often complained about a lack of male suitors. To rectify the problem, she'd head out to the suburban home of her co-worker Rob Petrie and his wife, Laura. There, in the more relaxed environment of New Rochelle, New York, Sally felt better about herself and was willing to accept flowers from strangers whom the Petries kindly set-up as her blind dates. *Courtesy of CBS-TV.*

season, the series was retitled *Archie's Place*. When the show ended its long run, it also featured such ethnic roles as that of an Irish cook, a Puerto Rican busboy, and a black housekeeper.

# Suburban New York

## The Dick Van Dyke Show

Rob Petrie (Dick Van Dyke), his wife, Laura (Mary Tyler Moore), and their son, Ritchie, lived at 448 Bonnie Meadow Road in New Rochelle, New York. This Westchester County town has long been a "bedroom community" whose breadwinners make the daily commute to and from their jobs in New York City. The setting for this classic sitcom, which featured Van Dyke as the head writer of the fictitious *Alan Brady Show*, was no accident. When asked about the inspiration behind the show, its creator, Carl Reiner, responded: "I remember exactly where it happened—it was on 96th Street by the East River in New York. I was driving my car downtown from New Rochelle . . ." Not only did Reiner live in New Rochelle; his house actually was on Bonnie Meadow Drive. He changed his address by one number for the Petries' address.

Although the Petries will forever be linked with suburbia, they didn't start out there. Rob and Laura met while he was in the army and stationed at Camp Crowder in Joplin, Missouri. After his discharge, they moved to Ohio, where they lived for a couple of years before settling in New Rochelle. *The Dick Van Dyke Show* ran from 1961 through 1966.

*Facing page:* A primitive form of cellular telephone kept agent Maxwell Smart (a.k.a. Don Adams) in touch with C.O.N.T.R.O.L. headquarters at 123 Main Street, Washington, D.C.   *Courtesy of Republic Pictures.*

# WASHINGTON, D.C.

Just as America keeps sending politicians to Washington, D.C., and is generally disappointed with what they do there, so Hollywood keeps setting shows in the nation's capital and (with a few notable exceptions) has been likewise generally disappointed with the results.

The first such series was *Mr. Smith Goes to Washington*, which was based on the Jimmy Stewart movie of the same name. In the TV version, Fess Parker (once *Davy Crockett* and yet to be *Daniel Boone*) played a United States senator elected from an unnamed state. His term in office lasted only for the 1962–63 season.

In *The Farmer's Daughter* (1963–66), Inger Stevens played Katy Holstrum, a Minnesota farm girl who goes to Washington to run the household affairs of a widowed congressman. The show was so popular with real politicos that when Katy married the congressman (William Windom) in 1965, Washington's premier hostess, Perle Mesta, staged a celebration. The guest list numbered 300 and both Stevens and Windom attended the party.

Secret agent Maxwell Smart, played by Don Adams, was the star of *Get Smart*. He reported to C.O.N.T.R.O.L. It was the headquarters of the only national security organization dumb enough to employ someone as stupid as Smart, with headquarters in a secret, subterranean command center. In the show's opening, we watch him enter a building, then a phone booth, then follow him down a descending elevator, and finally down stairs where, some ten floors beneath the city, he finally reaches his destination. C.O.N.T.R.O.L., at 123 Main Street in Washington, D.C., is the only covert agency to ever list its address in the phone book. *Get Smart* was decommissioned in 1970.

Two decades after serving as one-half of TV Land's first and only pair of identical cousins, Patty Duke starred in *Hail to the Chief* and came to Washington as the country's first female president. Her term lasted only for a couple of months, in 1985, before public dissatisfaction brought about her downfall. Ted Bessell, who had once been Anne Marie's boyfriend in *That Girl*, played the chief executive's philandering husband.

George C. Scott was the next resident of the White House. His series, *Mr. President*, did somewhat better than its predecessor as it endured from May of 1987 until April of 1988. This sitcom featured Conrad Bain (the former Philip Drummond of *Diff'rent Strokes*) as a presidential aide and Madeline Kahn as the surrogate First Lady.

*Top of the Hill* was a one-hour political drama about idealistic U.S. Representative Thomas Bell. Bell was played by William Katt, the former *Greatest American Hero* and the real-life son of *Perry Mason* star Barbara Hale. Congressman Bell's term in office was very short-lived, as the series ended within two months of its September 1989 inaugural episode.

*Murphy Brown*, the most honored and the most renowned Washington, D.C.–based series, debuted on November 14, 1988. Candice Bergen (daughter of ventriloquist Edgar Bergen) was cast in the title role of a Betty Ford Clinic graduate and journalist who hosts a TV news magazine show. *Murphy Brown* became involved with real-life politics during the 1992 presidential elections when Vice President Dan Quayle assailed the character for giving birth to a baby out of wedlock. While Quayle was subsequently voted out of office, Murphy scored big in the Nielsen ratings and was rewarded with another network renewal for her good work.

*The FBI.* After the detective agency (77 Sunset Strip) went belly-up, Efrem Zimbalist, Jr., shed his Stu Bailey P.I. persona and moved to Washington, D.C., where he got a job with the Feds and changed his name to Inspector Erskine. Have badge will bust. *Courtesy of ABC-TV.*

# EASTERN TV LAND GRAVE SITES

## New York

| | | |
|---|---|---|
| Rod Serling | 1924–75 | Interlaken Cemetery Interlaken, N.Y. |
| Dorothy Kilgallen | 1913–65 | Gates of Heaven Mt. Pleasant, N.Y. |
| Ed Sullivan | 1901–74 | Ferncliff Mausoleum Hartsdale, N.Y. |
| Moms Mabley | 1894–75 | Ferncliff Cemetery Hartsdale, N.Y. |

## Connecticut

| | | |
|---|---|---|
| Raymond Massey | 1896–1983 | Beaverdale Cemetery New Canaan, Conn. |

## Massachusetts

| | | |
|---|---|---|
| John Belushi | 1949–82 | Abel's Hill Cemetery Chilmark, Mass. |

# EASTERN TV LAND GEOGRAPHIA

## Offshore

TV Land's expansion has not always been in a westerly direction. Its borders were first extended offshore, to the east, by *The Pruitts of Southampton* in September of 1966. Phyllis Diller reigned as a Long Island socialite who had lost her millions to the IRS. The series changed its format and its name to *The Phyllis Diller Show* in January of 1967, when John Astin (a.k.a. Gomez Addams), Marty Ingels (the Fenster to Astin's Dickens in *I'm Dickens, He's Fenster*), and Gypsy Rose Lee were added to the cast.

*Wings*, another sitcom, is set on the island of Nantucket, off Massachusetts. Tim Daly plays the co-owner of a one-airplane airline based at the island's Tom Nevers Field. *Wings* debuted in April of 1990.

## Urban Cowpoke

The East was the East and the West was the West . . . up until the fall of 1970, that is. That's when *McCloud*, a deputy marshall played by Dennis Weaver (once known as Chester, of Dodge City), came riding into New York City from Taos, New Mexico. He was in New York on assignment to learn the methodology employed by big-city crime fighters. Deputy Marshall Sam was sure glad he hadn't left his horse and saddle behind, because pursuing criminals down heavily trafficked Fifth Avenue proved more effective on horseback than it was behind the wheel of a squad car. The show ran until late in the summer of 1977.

*McCloud* returned, in a TV movie of the week, in November of 1989. In *The Return of Sam McCloud*, McCloud had gotten off his high horse and had become a political animal. The hard-riding, cowboy-hatted lawman from Taos was a different kind of lawman this time around. Sam had been elected a United States senator.

## From the Back of the Cave to the Stars

Whenever Buck Rogers blasted off into outer space, he was being mission-controlled from a secret command post hidden in a cave located behind Niagara Falls. If you asked Buck (Robert Pastene), he'd say the year was 2430. *Buck Rogers*, however, took flight only

*The Howdy Doody Show.* From December 1947 till January 1956, freckle-faced Howdy, Buffalo Bob, Clarabelle the clown (who later became Captain Kangaroo), and the rest of the show's cast resided in Doodyville, Texas. All the kids in town had seats in what was called the Peanut Gallery. This community of juvenile fans, marionettes, and the people who pulled their strings remains as lost to modern civilization as the continent of Atlantis.
*Courtesy of NBC-TV.*

between April of 1950 and January of 1951. Gil Gerard starred as Buck in a short-lived series entitled *Buck Rogers in the 25th Century* (1979–81).

## Treasures

The Smithsonian Institution in Washington, D.C., often called "the nation's attic," has an eclectic representation of TV Land artifacts. They include Archie and Edith Bunker's living room chairs from *All in the Family*; Fonzie's leather jacket from *Happy Days*; a *Barney Miller* coffee cup; a tent from *M★A★S★H★*; *The Waltons'* radio; and the original *Felix the Cat* model, which was one of the first images ever to appear on an American TV screen.

The Museum of Television and Radio in New York contains the world's largest repository of TV shows that are available for viewing on videotape. The archives of TV history are found here in an environment that seeks to accommodate both casual visitors and scholars of the subject. The museum is at 25 West 52nd Street. Call them for current visiting hours and the cost of admittance at (212)624-6600.

The American Museum of the Moving Image (AMMI) is located at 35th Avenue and 36th Street in the Astoria section of Queens. It's filled with more than 70,000 TV and movie artifacts. Here, for example, is TV Land's greatest collection of Bill Cosby's TV sweaters. The museum is open from noon to 4 P.M. Tuesday through Friday; noon to 6 P.M. on weekends; closed Mondays. To check on their current exhibitions, call (718)784-4520.

# REALLY GOING TO—

## CHEERS

Cheers, according to the TV show of the same name, is a tavern in Boston run by a former Red Sox pitcher named Sam "Mayday" Malone. One of television's longest-running sitcoms (1982–93), its cast included Ted Danson as Sam, Rhea Perlman as barmaid Carla Tortelli, Shelley Long as barmaid Diane Chambers, Woody Harrelson as a bartender, John Ratzenberger and George Wendt as barflies Cliff and Norm, Kelsey Grammer as psychiatrist Dr. Frasier Crane, Bebe Neuwirth as his psychoanalytic wife, Dr. Lilith Sternin Crane, and Kirstie Alley as bar manager Rebecca Howe.

While Sam Malone and his cohorts are all fic-

Kirstie Alley played Rebecca Howe, the sultry and stuck-up character who took over as manager of Cheers in 1987. The Cheers bar is a true Boston landmark, located in the city's Back Bay section, but is known as the Bull & Finch in the real world.
*Courtesy of NBC -TV.*

tional characters, the bar itself is real. Occupying the very same location in the Back Bay district as its TV version, 84 Beacon Street, directly opposite the Public Gardens, is the Bull & Finch. Located a flight of steps down from street level, it has the brick walls, diamond-shaped windows, Tiffany-style lamps, and mahogany bar seen duplicated on TV. Approximately one million people each year come in search of TV Land's most popular bar—a figure that rivals many of Boston's most historical sites.

For those unable to make the pilgrimage to Boston, opportunities exist to visit plasticized versions of the Cheers bar in airports serving the cities of St. Louis, Kansas City, Minneapolis, Cleveland, Detroit, Anchorage, and Christchurch, New Zealand. These airport Cheers facsimiles are not franchises of the Bull & Finch: they're a part of Host International, a division of the Marriott hotel chain.

A kind of quirky portal into TV Land, intended to attract frequent-flier types who are likely to be couch potatoes at home, they replicate the look of the original but can't—and don't—come anywhere near the original as far as ambiance is concerned. They do, however, try to be familiar in a most unusual way.

Two familiar-looking gents are to be found, sitting at each of these airport Cheers bars, exhibiting repetitive behavior. There's a definite sequence to their actions: they lean into the bar, they sit up straight, they look each other in the eye, they engage in what appears to be happy talk. People entering the bars notice the two barflies right away, approach them, and try to edge into their conversation. As they do, the two drinking buddies start slouching toward the bar again.

They look a lot like Cheers' best customers, Norm and Cliff. They would, in fact, be exact doubles of TV's most famous tipplers, and would go by the same names, but legal and contractual issues prevent such complete duplication. These two fellows are real dummies—truly animated figures—to wit, they are robots!

# Sesame Place

Perhaps more dynamic than Howdy Doody's Doodyville ever was, maybe more neighborly than even Mr. Rogers's Neighborhood may have been, is that kiddies' corner of TV Land through which runs *Sesame Street*. No TV show revolutionized children's television more than this one. Since its inception in November of 1969, *Sesame Street* has entertained and educated millions of kids with ingenious creativity. Music, animation, skits, and graphics are combined with live hosts and a cast of immortal puppets. Originally aimed at urban pre-scholars, the show has won the hearts and minds of parents as well as their children. Its audience is representative of every economic and social level. No one who has seen the show has ever failed to be charmed and impressed with its content and execution. Considering the show's fame and the fabulous affection that millions have for it, it's only natural that there's a place in TV Land for its most well-known personality, Big Bird, to nest. This kids' best fine-feathered friend is, indeed, well sheltered (along with cohorts Bert, Ernie, Grover, Elmo, the Cookie Monster, and other *Street* denizens) at Sesame Place.

Sesame Place the theme park is a nine-acre puppetized paradise located in Langhorne, Pennsylvania, about thirty minutes north of Philadelphia. Its top attractions include Sesame Island, a play area as well as entertainment center with a tropical look; Sesame Neighborhood, a replica of the TV show's set; Ernie's Waterworks, a water ride playground; Sesame Food Factory; and Oscar's Trash Can Bandstand. The most active area of all is called Twiddlebug Land. The Twiddles are those creatures who live in the flowerbox outside of Bert and Ernie's window. Twiddlebug Land is the world seen from their point of view. It has a 10,000-square-foot wave pool upon which visitors float beneath a leaky, seven-foot-long garden-hose noz-zle; an oversized wristwatch with a band that doubles as a slide; a six-teen-foot-high sand-filled pail to mess with; the Mix-N-Match Twiddle Tracks railroad to ride; and an educational vegetable garden maze to explore.

Sesame Place is open daily except for its weekend-only policy from mid-September through mid-October. For admission prices, detailed directions, and lodging in-formation, call (215) 752-7070.

The Real McCoys
(origin)

Walton's
Mountain
(Schuyler)

(Pixley)
*The Beverly
Hillbillies*
(Hooterville)
*Petticoat Junction
Green Acres*

*Dukes of
Hazzard*

West
Virginia

Virginia

Mayberry
(Mount Airy)

*Daniel Boone*
(Trinity)

Kentucky

North Carolina

OZARK
MOUNTAINS

*Evening
Shade*

*Hee Haw*
(Nashville)

Tennessee

Swamp Fox

Arkansas

South Carolina

Popeye
(Alma)

Mississippi

*The Rebel*
(origin)

Carter Country
(near Plains)

Georgia

Louisiana

*In the Heat
of the Night*

Alabama

*Tallahassee 7000*

*Flamingo Road*

(New Orleans)
*Bourbon Street Beat
Yancy Derringer
Frank's Place
Longstreet
Maverick
Jim Bowie*

Florida

*I Dream of
Jeannie*
(Cocoa Beach)

*Gentle
Ben*

*Flipper*

(Miami/
Miami Beach)
*Miami Vice
Surfside Six
The Golden Girls*

N
W        E
S

# SOUTHERN TV LAND

One of the earliest introductions to the southern region of TV Land was in the autumn of 1959 by *The Swamp Fox*. Part of *Walt Disney Presents*, this six-episode saga was the story of General Francis Marion, played by Leslie Nielsen. It wasn't just a history lesson, it was a geography lesson as well. General Marion, using his nom de guerre, waged behind-enemy-lines guerrilla warfare throughout the Carolinas against the British during the American Revolution. The Carolina colonies were filled with leafy forests, as well as rich and rolling farmland. It was also cut by a lot of rivers and, of course, contained great patches of swampland.

Another series, *Daniel Boone*, which began in September of 1964 and ran to 1970, likewise defined the region. Daniel was portrayed by Fess Parker, who had previously established himself as Davy Crockett. He blazed a trail over the Cumberland Gap and into the wooded slopes and bluegrass meadows of Kentucky. Boone showed us the majesty of the Appalachians and the beauty of the unsettled American frontier. Daniel didn't like it when a place got filled up with settlers. Insisting that he had to have "elbow room," he kept picking up stakes and pioneering on. *Daniel Boone* exemplified the concept of Manifest Destiny—the nation's relentless drive to expand from the eastern seaboard to the Mississippi River and beyond. Helping Boone to extend the American empire were such cast members as country star Jimmy Dean and football great Roosevelt Grier. Angela Cartwright, who had once played Danny Thomas's daughter in *Make Room for Daddy* and was later to be Penny Robinson in *Lost in Space*, portrayed Boone's daughter, Jemima.

Just as *The Swamp Fox* was linked to the Carolinas and *Daniel Boone* to Kentucky, it was *The Real McCoys* (1957–62) that put West Virginia on the map. The McCoys, or so the show's theme song told us, were from "West Virginnie," though they moved to Southern California's San Fernando Valley. Walter Brennan was Grandpa Amos McCoy and Richard Crenna was his grandson, Luke. Butch Patrick, who went on to become Eddie Munster of *The Munsters*, was a cast member during the 1963–64 season.

Following *The Real McCoys* from the south to the west were *The Beverly Hillbillies* (1962–71), but not before they briefly introduced us to the Ozark Mountains. The show's opening sequence gave us a glimpse of the kind of terrain where Jed Clampett (played by Buddy Ebsen, who had been Davy Crockett's sidekick) went squirrel hunting and under which lay

Buddy Ebsen played Jed Clampett, a man who gave up hillbilly life when he moved his clan from the Ozarks to California but didn't forsake life in the hills entirely. The mansion seen in the series isn't located in the "flats" of Beverly Hills where Burns and Allen lived, but is rather fittingly set in the hilly area above Sunset Boulevard known as Bel-Air. *Courtesy of Viacom.*

crude oil. The oil made Jed a millionaire and they all abandoned their Ozark Mountain Pixley home for Beverly Hills. TV historians point out that the Hillbillies' hometown is also known by the names of Sibley and Bud Blossom. The Clampett truck is currently parked at the Folk Art Museum in Branson, Missouri.

The Clampetts left kin behind in the region. They were related to the folks of *Petticoat Junction* (1963–70), which was set in the community of Hooterville, home of the Shady Rest Inn. Former cowboy sidekick Smiley Burdette was part of a cast, which included Sharon Tate during the 1963–64 season. The greater Hooterville area was also the setting of *Green Acres* (1965–71). It was in Hooterville that a sophisticated Manhattan couple (Eddie Albert and Eva Gabor as Oliver Wendell Douglas and his wife Lisa) bought a farm, and where their most intelligent neighbor was a pig named Arnold Ziffel. Getting to *Green Acres*, according to Lisa Douglas, was no problem. "You just have to change planes twice," she said, "then take a bus from the county seat to Pixley and take a little train to Hooterville."

Attention in this southern region would later turn to bigger towns and more modern lifestyles—to the town of Truro (*Flamingo Road*) and to Sparta, Mississippi (*In The Heat of the Night*); to *Evening Shade*, Arkansas, and to Atlanta, city of *Designing Women*. But before it did, *The Dukes of Hazzard* established their namesake county, in Georgia, on the TV Land map. The Dukes (Catherine Bach, Tom Wopat, John Schneider, and Denver Pyle, among others) took us roaring down Hazzard County's back roads in the General Lee race car. Hot rods, as well as accents, were featured regional hallmarks. Southern TV Land, however, could never be better identified as a region unto itself than it was by the very sound of the names of many of the show's characters: Boss and Big Daddy and Buster, Enos and Cletus, Lulu and Cooter and Hughie Hogg. *The Dukes of Hazzard* ran from January of 1979 through August of 1985.

# NEW ORLEANS

New Orleans, the Queen City of the Mississippi River, is a place of charm and personality, and has been the setting for a variety of TV series. Jock Mahoney was *Yancy Derringer* (1958–59). He was a New Orleans dandy; the man who kept a miniature pistol, a gun that now bears his name, in his hat. Other cast members were Frances Bergen, who played the Miss Kitty–like Madame Francine, and X Brands, who was Yancy's Indian buddy Pahoo.

Two other New Orleans men of erudition were detectives Randolph and Calhoun, played by Richard Long and Andrew Duggan, respectively. Their series was called *Bourbon Street Beat* (1959–60). Shot on the Hollywood set of *A Streetcar Named Desire*, *Beat* also went on location in New Orleans, using the second floor of the city's Absinthe House restaurant as the "authentic" setting for the offices of the private detective agency.

*Longstreet* was another New Orleans prototype investigator; a blind insurance investigator who worked his job with the help of his Seeing Eye dog, Pax. James Franciscus, the former *Mr. Novak*, played Michael Longstreet from September of 1971 through August of 1972.

*Frank's Place* (1987–88) was a TV show about the fictitious Chez Louisiane restaurant. It was modeled on the city's real Chez Helene. Created by Hugh Wilson, the producer who also gave us *WKRP in Cincinnati*, *Frank's Place* starred Tim Reid as the man who inherits the eatery from his father.

# FLORIDA

Florida is best known as the domain for a domesticated dolphin, a female genie, sassy senior citizens, and Armani-suited vice-fighters. Fictitious Coral Keys State Park was the home of *Flipper* (1964–67). Cocoa Beach, a real town near the Cape Canaveral space base, was the setting for *I Dream of Jeannie*, a truly spacy series

Jeannie has always dwelled in a sun-blessed part of the world. She was presumably born somewhere in Arabia, was discovered by an astronaut named Major Nelson on an unnamed South Sea Isle, and was taken to his home in Cocoa Beach, Florida. She didn't use sunblock but thanks to network censors, never got her belly-button sunburned. *Courtesy of Screen Gems.*

which ran from 1965 to 1970. Astronaut Tony Nelson (Larry Hagman, prior to his J. R. Ewing days on *Dallas*) had discovered Jeannie, the genie, after his crash-landing on a desert island. Jeannie was played by Barbara Eden, who eventually changed her name to Stella Johnson, moved to Ohio, and joined the *Harper Valley PTA*. Miami was the home of *The Golden Girls* (1985–91). The girls, each of whom had graduated from middle age, lived together as roommates. The cast included Bea Arthur (formerly *Maude* of Tuckahoe, N.Y.) and Betty White (the former Sue Ann Nivens of Minneapolis and *The Mary Tyler Moore Show*). Miami was also urban battleground for detectives Crockett and Tubbs (Don Johnson and Philip Michael Thomas), who were the central characters in *Miami Vice*. The series ran from 1984 to 1989. Miami's ambiance—art deco architecture, blue skies, and the sea—were prominently featured, as the show filmed its exterior shots on location here. Among those to appear in this flashiest of all Florida-based shows were such guest stars as Bianca Jagger, Phil Collins, Lee Iacocca, Miles Davis, G. Gordon Liddy, Ted Nugent, Roberto Duran, Glenn Frey, and Leonard Cohen.

Other Floridian series include: *Surfside Six* (set in Miami Beach and starring Troy Donahue); *Tallahassee 7000* (set in the state capitol and starring Walter Matthau); *Miami Undercover* (with Rocky Graziano); *Michael Shayne* (set in Miami Beach and with Jerry Paris among its cast); *Caribe* (set in Miami and starring Stacy Keach); and *The Everglades* (set in the massively swampy Everglades County).

# SOUTHERN TV LAND GEOGRAPHIA

## Down-Home Hometown(s)

TV Land became a politically prophetic place, in September of 1977, when *Carter Country* began its run. Set in the town of Clinton Corners, Georgia—merely "a hoot and a holler" from the town of Plains—it was the first TV show to be named after a president who was currently in office. The series, whose cast included Melanie Griffith, didn't last as long as the Carter presidency. It was retired in 1979 after forty-three episodes, and twelve years before Bill Clinton was elected president.

## Gone Fishing

When Sheriff Andy Taylor and his boy Opie went fishing, as seen in the opening of every episode of *The Andy Griffith Show*, they headed for bucolic Myer's Lake. The lake, however, is nowhere near Mayberry. TV Land anglers are advised to look for it in Los Angeles' Franklin Canyon—an inside-the-city-limits wilderness that borders Beverly Hills. The lake is actually a pond, and no fish swim in its polluted waters.

# Treasures

There's a repository of reality in the heart of Southern TV Land. Thousands of hours of ABC, CBS, and NBC news broadcasts, from 1969 to the current day, are available for viewing on videotape at the Vanderbilt News Archive. No other such collection, including those of the networks themselves, rivals this one. The Archive is located at the 6th Stack in the Main Building at the Joint University Libraries at Vanderbilt University. The address is 419 21st Avenue South, Nashville, Tennessee. The phone number is (615)322-1927, and they're open from 9 A.M. to 6 P.M., Monday through Friday.

# REALLY GOING TO—

# Mayberry

Mayberry was the setting for *The Andy Griffith Show*. This gentle, cornpone series (1960–68) starred Griffith as Sheriff Andy Taylor, Ron Howard as his son Opie, Frances Bavier as Aunt Bee, Don Knotts as Deputy Barney Fife, and Jim Nabors as Gomer Pyle.

Unlike most sitcoms, *The Andy Griffith Show* has authentic roots in its setting. Griffith's boyhood home was in Mount Airy, North Carolina, and his hometown, close by the Great Smoky Mountains, came to serve as the real-life model for Mayberry. Despite signs of suburbanization indicated by the presence of such contemporary enterprises as Opie's Video Store in Mount Airy's Mayberry Mall, the town remains fairly unchanged, despite the three decades that have passed since the series premiered.

## How and What to Know When You're in Mayberry...
## and Not in Mount Airy

*Mayberry Population:* 2,400
*Mount Airy Population:* 7,200
*Speed Limit in Mayberry:* 20 miles per hour

# Banner Years in the History of Mayberry

1747—The community began with the establishment of a trading post, which served the surrounding area known as "The Hollows."

1885—Mount Airy is officially incorporated as a town.

1923—Snappy Lunch opens for business.

1927—Andy Griffith, age six, moves to town.

1944—Andy leaves home to attend the University of North Carolina in Chapel Hill.

1960—*The Andy Griffith Show* began airing on CBS.

1968—The final first-run episode of the show airs on CBS.

1969— *Mayberry, R.F.D.*, with Ken Berry, premieres.

# Walking Tour of Main Street in Mayberry

A short walking tour around town will bring any ambulatory fan of Andy, Opie, Barney, Aunt Bee, Gomer, Goober, Floyd, Emmet, Mayor Beamer, and the rest of Mayberry's immortal TV souls to the front doors of a variety of truly hallowed landmarks of TV Land.

### Snappy Lunch

Snappy Lunch is the only place to dine if you want to eat as well as live and breathe the Mayberry Experience. The tiny Main Street restaurant opened in 1923 and, according to owner/chef Charlie Dowell, "It was the closest thing to fast food we had then." Andy Griffith was a semi-regular patron back in the 1940s, when he was a student at Mount Airy High School. The school didn't have a cafeteria at the time and kids who didn't bring a sack lunch were allowed to go into town for their meals. Snappy Lunch was the closest place to go. Raymond Herrick, who co-owned the Snappy for a while, was one of Griffith's next-door neighbors.

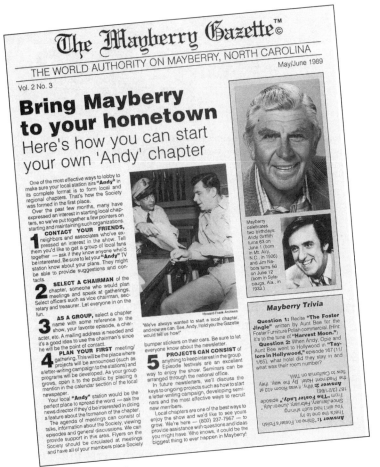

*Courtesy of John Meroney.*

In terms of its TV incarnation, Snappy Lunch was where Sheriff Andy Taylor went for lunch whenever Aunt Bee didn't make him some sandwiches to eat in his court house office. It was also where Andy and Barney would go to treat themselves to a cool glass of soda pop on a hot summer's evening.

T-shirts bearing the angelic faces of Andy, Opie, and Aunt Bee

Mayberry exists on multiple planes: it occupies a place in the hearts of millions; it's a lost American innocence state of mind; a former Culver City, California, TV studio backlot; and the town of Mount Airy, North Carolina. It's Mount Airy that you see here—obviously not as bucolic as the town you saw on TV. But there's much more to do in Mayberry/Mount Airy today. There's not only the Mayberry Mall (where Opie's Video store is found) but the Mayberry Motor Inn (which boasts the Aunt Bee Memorial), as well.
*Courtesy of Mount Airy, N.C., Chamber of Commerce.*

are sold here. And so are lots of pork chop sandwiches. The chops are extra-large and come dressed with homemade chili, mustard, coleslaw, tomato, and onions . . . really sloppy but, as Andy might say, "They're Mmm-mmm Mayberry good."

### Floyd's Barbershop

Right in the heart of downtown is the City Barbershop. Renamed Floyd's Barbershop on the show, this historic salon was essentially unchanged, in terms of ambiance, in its TV version. It still looks exactly like the place where Andy Griffith got his hair cut during his wonder years. And, even in these modern times, the real mayor is as likely to be occupying one of the barber chairs and holding court as Mayberry's fictional Mayor Beamer was. Owner/barber Russell Hiatt loves to tell old Andy stories to anyone who makes the pilgrimage to this bastion of local sartorial splendor. According to Russell, "Every person and every place in the show was based on someone or something that he [i.e. Andy] knew here in Mount Airy. There was Aunt Bee and the town drunk; why, that could have been any number of three or four guys. We got them, too, you know." Russell also has, on sale at his barbershop, T-shirts and caps that commemorate the contributions Mayberry has made to civilization.

**Lamm's Drugstore**
They don't sell any Mayberry souvenirs at Lamm's, but the place is worth a quick visit. It's a living museum of a pharmacy—with its antique scale, counters, and display cases. Not just the place where Andy's parents bought the kid cough medicine, Lamm's was the store where Sheriff Andy would visit girlfriend (played by a mature Princess, i.e., Elinor Donahue, whose royal role it was on *Father Knows Best*).

**Grace Moravian Church**
The church, which stands at the corner of North Main and Grace streets, wasn't mentioned on the show, but it figured prominently in the development of Andy Griffith's show business career. It was here that the young Griffith, not particularly athletic or scholarly, found he had some talent for making music. Griffith was sometimes seen and heard, in his role of Mayberry's Sheriff Taylor, while picking at his guitar and warbling a bit to his girlfriend as they sat on his front porch on a humid North Carolinian summer eve. As a kid, it was at the Grace Moravian that he learned to sing and play the trombone and entertain the Sunday faithful.

## Sights Around Town

A number of Mount Airy thoroughfares resurface in mythical Mayberry; Haymore and Rockford streets are worth cruising. Along them are . . .

The Andy Griffith Boyhood House, a simple clapboard home, which has been expanded over the years, is at 711 East Haymore Street on the south side of town.

The Rockford Street School, which Andy once attended, was torn down some twenty years ago or so. Its auditorium, however, was left standing. Renamed The Andy Griffith Playhouse, it now serves as a community theater.

The Mount Airy Furniture Company is where Andy's father, Carl, toiled during the family's years in residence here. The building still stands on Factory Street.

## Being with Aunt Bee

Mount Airy hasn't forgotten its First Lady. Aunt Bee's crucial importance in TV Land history is honored by The Aunt Bee Memorial. It occupies one of twenty-seven guest rooms in the Mayberry Motor Inn. Pictures of her adorn the walls. Bee (known as Frances Bavier beyond the borders of TV Land) would feel at home here. All the memorial's furnishings were bought from her estate after her death in 1991.

## Mayberry: Home of the Stars

Andy Griffith wasn't the first celebrity to ever call the marvelous Mayberry mini-metropolitan area home. Country music star Donna Fargo was born in Mount Airy in 1927. The Mayberry/Show Business Connection dates even further back than that.

It was in 1839 that two inseparable and world-famous stars of the Barnum and Bailey Circus, Siamese twins Chang and Eng, visited this area and liked it so much that they settled down. The men, who were thirty-four years old at the time, married a pair of local sisters and built separate homes for each of their wives. The men divided their time between the two places by spending three days in one home before moving on to the second for the following three days. They were at Eng's house when they died at the age of

69, within minutes of one another. Eng's house burned down in 1950, but Chang's place can still be seen just south of town.

To visit their graves, in the cemetery of the White Plains Baptist Church, leave Mount Airy by taking U.S. 601 south. The church is about five miles from town.

# Walton's Mountain

**WALTON'S MOUNTAIN MUSEUM**

The Schuyler Community Center on Walton's Mountain

*Schuyler, Virginia in Nelson County*

Located in the foothills òf the Blue Ridge Mountains (approximately 140 miles northeast of Mount Airy, North Carolina) is the town of Schuyler, Virginia. Just as Mount Airy came to be recast as Mayberry, Schuyler (located in central Virginia's Nelson County) became famous as the setting for *The Waltons*, TV Land's most celebrated family circa the Great Depression. Schuyler, which has a population of four hundred, is the hometown of the series' creator, Earl Hamner, Jr. As Hamner's creation is distinctly (if disguisedly) autobiographical, Schuyler's townsfolk, its institutions, and its social history were reflected in the series.

*The Waltons* network run was from the fall of 1972 through August of 1981. Its large cast included Will Geer as Grandpa Zeb; Ralph Waite as John Walton; Michael Learned as John's wife,

Olivia; and Richard Thomas as John-Boy Walton. John-Boy, an aspiring writer, provided the narrative voice of the show.

## A Place for Memories

When the town's elementary school closed in 1990, it prompted a proposal to establish a museum in the empty building. Money to create the Walton's Mountain Museum was provided by a $30,000 grant from the state of Virginia, a $10,000 donation made by Earl Hamner, Jr., and $10,000 collected from a local fund-raising drive. Lorimar Productions, which produced the show, was willing to donate the sets, but they were destroyed in a fire.

The plans for the sets were lost. Undaunted, the museum's planners studied the show's sets carefully and built duplicates. They dressed the sets with authentic period furnishings found throughout the central Virginia area.

After eighteen months of planning and construction, the museum opened on October 24, 1992. Five thousand fans came to town for the event. The all-day affair featured tours and speeches made by cast members, Hamner, and members of the Hamner family who still live in the region.

## The Walton's Mountain Museum

Occupying four rooms of the old school building are sets that recreate the world of the Walton family. They include John-Boy's bedroom; the icebox and wood stove–furnished kitchen; the living room with its antique foot-pump organ; and Ike Godsey's General Store.

An additional room is used to show a fifty-four-minute audio-visual program composed of videotaped interviews with some of the show's actors, writers, and directors. Also on display are hundreds of scripts, a case filled with Walton dolls, magazines with

Earl Hamner *(seated, foreground)* visits family members who were the prototypes for the Waltons, at his boyhood home in the Blue Ridge Mountains *Courtesy of CBS-TV.*

Walton covers, and various plaques honoring the show as well as the Emmy Award Earl Hamner, Jr., received for *The Waltons.* Expansion plans call for adding the set of the Baldwin sisters' parlor—the room in which they concocted their moonshine-based "Papa's Recipe" elixir.

The museum is open daily (10 A.M. to 4 P.M.) through the spring, summer, and fall but closes down for the winter season—from late November until early in March.

## Also Found in Town

There are four strictly unofficial sites to see in Schuyler that draw interest from die-hard fans. They are Luke Snead's country store (the model for Ike Godsey's); the Schuyler Baptist Church; the Hamner family home (where Earl, Jr.'s, mother is still in residence); and the local honky-tonk, which changes its name every couple of years and which inspired the show's Dew-Drop Inn.

# Evening Shade

*Evening Shade* is the reason why the state of Arkansas is now part of TV Land. A sitcom about life in a Southern town, its all-star cast includes Burt Reynolds, Marilu Henner, Hal Holbrook, Charles Durning, Elizabeth Ashley, Michael Jeter, and Ossie Davis. The show premiered in 1990.

Just as Andy Griffith and Earl Hamner, Jr., drew upon their roots to create Mayberry and Walton's Mountain, so too did the creators of this series. The husband and wife team of Harry Thomason and Linda Bloodworth-Thomason are natives of the rural South. Harry's from Hampton, Arkansas, and Linda was born in Poplar Bluff, Missouri, just a few miles north of the Arkansas border.

Anyone planning to visit Evening Shade ought to be aware that there are several towns in Arkansas with this name. There's one in Hempstead County with a population of less than fifty (120 miles from Little Rock); one in Scott County (also 120 miles from Little Rock); and a third one (240 miles from Little Rock) in Sharp County. It's the third one that is generally acknowledged to belong to TV Land.

Set in the rolling foothills of the Ozark Mountains, graced with rivers and a man-made lake, the Sharp County town is a bucolic place, but it isn't depicted on television as being particularly remote from the contemporary world. Located on U.S. 167, Evening Shade lies between the towns of Ash Flat and Cave City—and just a few hills away from Calamine.

Harry Thomason, however, hedges on the matter of which community is the true Evening Shade. "Both Linda and I," he once told the press, "know that there is another Evening Shade located in south Arkansas near Hope, where the world's largest watermelons are grown, so we decided to make our show a compendium of all Evening Shades." Still, it's the one in Sharp County that gets all the attention.

## All "D" Facts

*Differences, Distinctions, Disparities, and Distortions*
While no community in TV Land is an exact double of its real-life counterpart, the real and the mythical Evening Shades are the most dissimilar of all such pairings.

*Evening Shade, TV Land*
*Population:* 10,000
*Profile:* This town has a courthouse, a hospital, professional offices, and taverns.


*Dining and Race:* The favorite place to dine is Ponder Blue's Barbecue Villa, a local eatery owned by the character played by Ossie Davis.
Has a high school football team

*Evening Shade, Arkansas*
*Population:* 379
*Profile:* This town has a bank, four gas stations, a general store, and a mini-mart. There are no bars; the town is in a "dry" county.
*Dining and Race:* The local eatery is called The White Owl. There are no black residents of the town.

Has no football team.

# Going, Going, Gone to Town

Evening Shade has been visited by the show's co-executive producers as well as by actors Jay R. Ferguson and Michael Jeter. Burt Reynolds delivered the high school's 1991 commencement address. Cast member Charlie Dell accepted the town's invitation to hold his wedding in Evening Shade and did, indeed, get married there.

Still, the link between the mythical and the geographical realities of the place is tenuous. Really confusing the matter is the fact that the show's opening scenes depict a town that isn't Evening Shade! Still, visitors have arrived here from Canada, Mexico, South America, China, Japan, Europe, and each of the fifty states in the Union.

If you've resolved to pay a visit, head for Graddy's General Store. It's considered to be the unofficial visitor's center, and proprietor Fayon Graddy can be helpful. You can also buy caps, T-shirts, and sweatshirts there, which are emblazoned with the town's name.

# Investing in Evening Shade

The Evening Shade School Foundation raises funds for the establishment of a senior center and a new gym/auditorium for the high school by marketing (with the help of a Burt Reynolds's TV public service announcement) *The Evening Shade Cookbook*. Published by the Future Homemakers of America, its recipes include contributions from the show's cast. The foundation also sells T-shirts to raise money for a club for local teenagers. For current prices or to place an order, write to:

> The Evening Shade School Foundation, P.O. Box 36, Evening Shade, Arkansas 72532. Or, call them (but only while school is in session) at (501)266-3590.

# Dick Clark's American Bandstand Grill

Dick Clark, who is perhaps the most recognizable person in all of TV Land, was the host of *American Bandstand*—the dance show that managed to run for decades. While Dick went on to create, host, and produce numerous TV game shows, network and syndicated series, and specials, it was *Bandstand* that made it all possible for him.

The show, broadcast from a studio in Philadelphia, is off the air, but continues its run on video monitors that play 100 hours' worth of tapes (1958 through 1989) in Dick Clark's American Bandstand Grill. This restaurant, in Miami's Bayside Market Place, has replicated the old Philly TV studio dance floor as well. Decorations include Mick Jagger's jacket, Elton John's hat, Bo Diddley's guitar, a surfboard that once belonged to the Beach Boys, and a doll that was thoroughly mutilated by Alice Cooper.

Hamburgers, pizza, sandwiches, and shakes are the main fare. Besides selling food and rock and roll nostalgia, the Grill also markets *Bandstand* souvenirs ranging from $3.00 visors to $185 *Bandstand* bomber jackets.

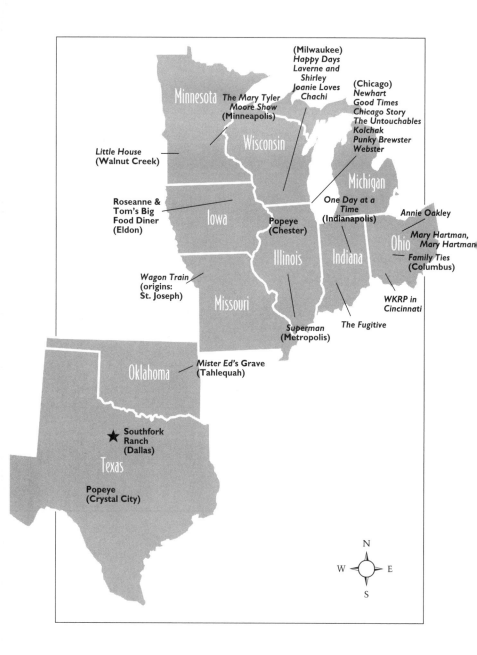

Minnesota

**(Milwaukee)**
*Happy Days*
*Laverne and*
*Shirley*
*Joanie Loves*
*Chachi*

The Mary Tyler
Moore Show
(Minneapolis)

Wisconsin

**(Chicago)**
*Newhart*
*Good Times*
*Chicago Story*
*The Untouchables*
*Kolchak*
*Punky Brewster*
*Webster*

Little House
(Walnut Creek)

Michigan

Roseanne &
Tom's Big
Food Diner
(Eldon)

Iowa

One Day at a
Time
(Indianapolis)

Annie Oakley

Popeye
(Chester)

Ohio

Mary Hartman,
Mary Hartman

Illinois

Indiana

Family Ties
(Columbus)

Wagon Train
(origins:
St. Joseph)

Missouri

WKRP in
Cincinnati

Superman
(Metropolis)

The Fugitive

Mister Ed's Grave
(Tahlequah)

Oklahoma

★ Southfork
Ranch
(Dallas)

Texas

Popeye
(Crystal City)

N
W — E
S

# CENTRAL TV LAND

Central TV Land used to be a decidedly mythical region. Its towns were as generic as much as they were imaginary. Most places, like Centerville, which could be Anywhere, USA, were probably located here. Centerville was the setting of one of the earliest sitcoms, *The Aldrich Family* (1949–53). This classic series featured several guest appearances by Paul Newman during its last season.

There was a certain, inviting commonality about this region's towns during the fifties and sixties. Most people, for example, lived in houses that had big backyards, though Dobie Gillis (*The Many Loves of Dobie Gillis*) was an exception. The Gillis family lived above their grocery store in Central City.

Trees grew all throughout the region, and people lived on streets named after them. Dobie's pal, Maynard G. Krebs, lived at 1343 South Elm Street in Central City. The Andersons, of *Father Knows Best* (1954–63), lived at 607 South Maple Street in Springfield. *Dennis the Menace* (1959–63) lived at 627 Elm Street in Hillsdale. Hillsdale was also the setting of *The Donna Reed Show*

*Father Knows Best.* The Andersons of Springfield were the idealized TV Land clan of the 1950s. Father (Robert Young) went on to become Marcus Welby, M.D. Betty (a.k.a. Princess), the eldest child, was played by Elinor Donahue. She later resurfaced in Mayberry on *The Andy Griffith Show,* then in New York City on *The Odd Couple.*    *Courtesy of CBS-TV.*

(1958–66). The Cleavers, of *Leave It to Beaver* (1957–63), resided at 211 Pine Street in Mayfield. Though it would seem highly unlikely, Ward Cleaver may have been trying to avoid the I.R.S. or was part of the Federal Witness Protection Program, because a title search of the Cleaver property lists addresses for them at Mapleton Drive and Lakewood Avenue as well as the one on Pine Street.

Central lifestyle exemplified TV Land's family values. Kids had chores to do. Parents slept in separate beds. Neighbors were neighborly. Nobody took Prozac, which, like TV zappers and call waiting and bar-code pricing, didn't yet exist. Life didn't get much better anywhere else than it did here during the so-called Golden Days of Television.

One woman and one town changed all that in the autumn of 1976. Mary Hartman, Mary Hartman was her name, was her name. Norman Lear, who was responsible for bringing *All in the Family, The Jeffersons, Maude,* and *Good Times* to television, brought us to Mary's absolutely unreal hometown of Fernwood, Ohio.

# CENTRAL TV LAND

The town may be mythical but the brilliant satire that was the hallmark of this series was utterly genuine. Things happened here that didn't happen anywhere else in the Central region before. Fernwood was the scene of action for a hostage-taking mass-murderer, a flasher, and a child evangelist who touched the hand of God when a TV fell in his bathtub and electrocuted him.

*Mary Hartman, Mary Hartman* was a serial and lasted for 325 episodes before concluding on July 3, 1977. During its year and a half of glory, its cast included Louise Lasser (as Mary), Dabney Coleman, Greg Mullavey, and Mary Kay Place. *Fernwood 2-Night* replaced *Mary Hartman, Mary Hartman* in the summer of 1977. This series satirized talk shows and starred Martin Mull as a local talk show host and Fred Willard as his sidekick. It ran from July until the end of September of 1977. *Forever Fernwood*, in turn, re-placed *Fernwood 2-Night*. This latest Fernwood-based show was es-sentially the same as *Mary Hartman, Mary Hartman*, with a title change due to the fact that Louise Lasser quit the title role. It ran through 1978.

Aside from the Fernwood phenomenon, the seventies was the era of big hit sitcoms set in the region's big cities. *The Mary Tyler Moore Show* was the name of one series and Minneapolis was the city in which it was set during its 1970 to 1977 run.

Minneapolis was chosen as the setting because, according to producer James L. Brooks, "it would trap the characters indoors." Brooks described the city as being "where the major industry is snow removal." Still, the opening shots of the show have served to establish two Minneapolis exterior locations as landmarks of TV Land. Lake of the Isles is where, in the show's opening, Mary Richards is seen feeding the ducks; Nicollet Mall is where she throws her hat up in the air.

Another big Central region hit series was the set-in-Chicago *Bob Newhart Show* (1972–76). *Good Times* (a spin-off of *Maude* starring John Amos, Esther Rolle, and Jimmie Walker) was also set in Chicago. It ran from 1974 through 1979. TV Land's flagship radio station, *WKRP in Cincinnati*, began broadcasting in 1978 and kept its signal going until 1982. The Romano family (Bonnie Franklin, Valerie Bertinelli, and Mackenzie Phillips) of *One Day at a Time* lived in Indianapolis from 1975 through 1984.

Milwaukee was the setting for *Happy Days*, which ran from 1974 through 1984. *Laverne and Shirley* was, likewise, a Milwaukee show from its inception in 1976 until 1980, when the girls moved to Burbank, California, for the three remaining years of their network run. *Family Ties*, in which Michael J. Fox starred as Alex Keaton, was set in Columbus, Ohio. It began in 1982 and ran for a full decade.

Before her life in Minneapolis, before life in New Rochelle, Mary Tyler Moore appeared on *Richard Diamond: Private Eye*. The pair of legs seen at the start of that show belonged to MTM, a star who didn't get to show her face until later in TV Land history. *Courtesy of NBC-TV.*

# CENTRAL TV LAND
## GEOGRAPHIA

## Sure, Annie's Got Her Gun

A life-size statue of Annie Oakley, Queen of the TV Cowgirls, stands in the Trapshooting Hall of Fame in Vandalia, Ohio.

## Mayberry in Ohio

Wally's Filling Station, the best gas station/garage in TV Land and the employer of Gomer Pyle until the time of his Marine Corps enlistment, can't be found in Mount Airy. It reincarnated, thanks to a fellow named Bob Scheib, in a Miami County, Ohio, cornfield. Bob began work on his own Wally's in the late 1980s and finished it in three years. Everything about it is identical to the original—the pumps, the building, the tools, the stock of fan belts and tires and motor oil, too. There's an antique soda pop machine selling bottles at Mayberry-era prices. Parked out front are four replicas of Sheriff Andy's cruisers. On the wall, just past the door, hangs a phone just like the one Wally had. On the wall beneath it are a series of scrawls: 371J; 247; 242. They're the phone numbers of Goober, Thelma Lou, and the Bluebird Diner.

Wally's Mayberry Filling Station in Ohio is at 10870 Circle Hill Road in Bradford, which is ten miles west of Troy, not too far from Cincinnati, and both hundreds of miles from and right next-door to Mayberry, North Carolina.

# Treasures

The Museum of Broadcast Communications and Electronic Media has extensive collections of TV-related material (including scripts, kinescopes, and videotapes). It's located in the Cultural Center, Washington Street and Michigan Avenue, Chicago, Illinois. They advise prospective visitors to call them at (312)629-6000 for directions, reservations, and current schedules and exhibitions. Admission is free.

*Facing page:* The city of Metropolis, Illinois, promotes itself as "Superman City." *Courtesy of Metropolis, Illinois, Chamber of Commerce.*

# REALLY GOING TO—

# Metropolis

The city of Metropolis will forever be linked with the character known as *Superman*. Originating in 1938 as a comic book hero, the Man of Steel got his own radio show in 1940. A couple of cartoon movie features and fifteen-minute movie serials followed, and then a theatrical release, *Superman and the Mole Men*, in 1951. 1951 also marked the start of production of the *Superman* TV series starring George Reeves in the title role, Phyllis Coates as Lois Lane, Jack Larson as Jimmy Olsen, and John Hamilton as Perry White. By the time it ceased in 1957, 104 episodes of this series had been produced.

**16th Annual**

**SUPERMAN CELEBRATION**

METROPOLIS, IL.

1994

HOME OF SUPERMAN

**Thursday-Sunday**

**June 9-12**

*Metropolis, Illinois*

*Debuting in 1994*

**Superman Comes Home**

CONVENTION

# Of Myth and Metropolis

Born on the planet Krypton and raised on a farm outside of Small-ville, it was the big city of Metropolis that eventually became Superman's (a.k.a. Clark Kent's) home. In truth, however, Metropolis (Metropolis, Illinois) has a population of about 7,000 people. The only town listed by this name in the U.S. Postal Directory, Metropolis officially proclaimed Superman as its hometown hero in 1972.

Seeking to capitalize on the municipality's link to the superhero, promoters worked to transform Metropolis into a tourist destination. Local citizens bought a quarter of a million dollars' worth of stock in a corporation formed to realize the commer-

Clark Kent is seen here in the guise of a very contemplative Superman. George Reeves, the actor who played the dual role, was probably contemplative as well: He committed suicide in his home in Benedict Canyon.
*Courtesy of Viacom.*

*Courtesy of DC Comics.*

*Courtesy of DC
Comics & "The
Metropolis Planet."*

cial venture. Plans were drawn to erect a combination theme park, museum, and shopping complex to be called "The Amazing World of Superman." Fifty thousand dollars was spent to license the Superman name.

The museum opened in a converted skating rink but was forced to close only three months later when the corporation went broke. Undaunted by this bankruptcy, the locals continued their attempts to exploit the economic potential of the Man of Steel. The chamber of commerce placed a commemorative talking telephone booth in its office and began handing out free samples of Kryptonite to visitors. The government renamed a street Lois Lane and dedicated Superman Square. Restaurants added Superman Specials to their menus and the town paper changed its name to *The Planet*.

Enormous likenesses of Superman were painted on a water tower and on what is billed as "the world's largest Superman billboard." A seven-foot fiberglass statue of Superman, wearing size twenty boots, used to stand outside the courthouse, on Superman Square. A new, fifteen-foot bronze statue took its place in June of 1993.

## Going to Metropolis

The best time to visit Metropolis is in July, during the annual Superman Celebration. It's a four-day event featuring a Superman road race, stamp exhibition, and the bestowing of the Lois Lane Award for community service.

# Roseanne and Tom's Big Food Diner

It used to be that anyone traveling through Iowa in search of TV Land was advised that they'd either have to settle for the next best thing or leave the state entirely. The next best thing was the "field of dreams"—the mythical baseball field set among rows of corn and brought to life by the movie of the same name. A true diamond in the rough, it has its charms, but TV Land it's not.

Iowa, however, became a province of TV Land on February 1, 1993, when Roseanne and Tom's Big Food Diner opened in the town of Eldon (population 1,070). This former wife and husband team, stars of the TV sitcoms *Roseanne* and *The Jackie Thomas Show*, went into the restaurant business after buying a 1700-acre ranch just outside of town.

Open from 6 A.M. until 9 P.M. seven days a week, the Big Food's fare might possibly appeal to someone who has been on a strict diet of frozen TV dinners for a lifetime. Instant mashed potatoes, chili, pork loins, and the house special called the "loose meat sandwich" are staples of the menu. The entrees, as you might surmise, aren't the diner's strongest draw. It's the ambiance that pulls in the crowds. With a seating capacity of fifty, the eatery is decorated in an appropriate TV Land motif.

Posters and photos of the two stars and their series' cast members decorate the walls. They lend an atmosphere of blue-collar glamour to an establishment that requires no reservations, with prices ranging from $1.50 to $4.50 a plate, where credit cards are not accepted, and in which high chairs are readily provided for visiting TV Land tots. The address is 101 Elm Street, Eldon, Iowa.

# Little House on the Prairie

*Little House on the Prairie* starred Michael Landon, Karen Grassle, Melissa Sue Anderson, and Melissa Gilbert. It ran from 1974 to 1982, and was very loosely based on Laura Ingalls Wilder's *On the Banks of Plum Creek*. According to this book and other Wilder books, Laura's father built his family a sod house on the banks of Plum Creek, a couple of miles north of Walnut Grove, Minnesota, in 1874. The creek, the plum trees that grow by it, the wildflowers, and the prairie that Laura described in her book are all still in evidence. The sod house is long gone, but its dugout foundation, called "the depression," remains.

Thanks to the Laura Ingalls Wilder Memorial Society, these sites have been protected and marked for TV Land tourists. The society's membership is strictly for book lovers, however, and they think the TV show is a joke. But TV-oriented *Little House* lovers can't be refused admittance to these landmarks. All they have to do is ante up the requested donation: $2.00 per car load, $10.00 per bus.

While the rural Plum Creek location is hallowed ground to the 25,000 fans who visit it each year, the *Little House* shrine is in town.

Occupying a former railroad depot, off Route 14, is the Laura Ingalls Wilder Museum. Its collection of documents, objects, and photographs gives a representative look at what life was like here in the closing decades of the nineteenth century. The only other historical remains of the local Ingalls family is the bell that hangs in the belfry of the English Lutheran Church. Laura's father contributed to its purchase.

## Where in TV Land Is It?

To see the Plum Creek homestead, take County Road 5 north from Walnut Creek to where a marker signals all Little House seekers to turn down a dirt road. Go past a soybean farm to a spot where you'll find a place to park and a lock-box in which to stuff donations. From there, it's a short walk to the Ingalls' old place, with its various spots (such as the Big Rock she played at and wrote about) indicated by painted wooden signs.

Walnut Creek is 150 miles southwest of Minneapolis. The Museum/Tourist Center is open spring, summer, and fall on a daily basis. Admission is free. Write to its curator at Box 58, Walnut Grove, Minnesota 56180. The telephone number is (502)859-2358.

# The Three Popeyes

Popeye the (pipe-smoking, spinach-eating, and tattooed) Sailor Man was created by cartoonist E. C. Segar and made his first public appearance in the Thimble Theater comic strip in 1929. He became a cartoon movie character in 1933, when he debuted in a black-and-white Betty Boop screen short. He was soon on his way to Arabia where three, two-reel Technicolor Popeye movies established him as a screen idol. Those films were *Popeye Meets Sinbad the Sailor*, *Popeye Meets Ali Baba and His Forty Thieves*, and *Popeye Meets Aladdin and His Wonderful Lamp*. The film shorts (of which over 250 were made) began appearing in TV syndication in 1958. Another 200 Popeye cartoons were produced for TV between 1961 and 1963 and have been continually rerun ever since their original airing.

It isn't for the Sailor Man's screen work but rather because of his unwavering identification with spinach that he's been honored with memorials. There's one in Crystal City, Texas. This community, which is south of San Antonio and close to the Rio Grande, has a population of 8,500 people. The site of a huge Del Monte cannery, Crystal City has been calling itself the Spinach Capital of the World since the 1930s. The town's focal point, and a principal source of its civic pride, is its statue of Popeye.

Alma, Arkansas (population 2,700), also claims to be the Spinach Capital of the World. It's the home of the Allen Canning Company. Allen began marketing Popeye brand spinach in 1967 and laid claim to Crystal City's title twenty years later. Like its

Texas competitor, Alma also boasts a statue of the Sailor Man to watch over the town.

There's yet another Popeye statue standing tall and proud in TV Land. This six-foot, bronzed Sailor Man is found in a small park overlooking the Mississippi River, near the Chester Toll Bridge, in Chester, Illinois—the hometown of E. C. Segar. Erected to honor Segar rather than to promote the marketing of spinach, this statue of the cartoon hero was dedicated on June 25, 1977. An annual Popeye Picnic, staged each September, celebrates TV Land's one-eyed, two-fisted spinach advocate with a carnival, rides, a parade, and a feast of spinach dishes . . . plus plenty of Wimpy-burgers.

# Southfork Ranch

With the possible exception of the Clampetts, the Ewing clan of *Dallas* was the wealthiest family in TV Land. They, too, made their money in oil, and it was their vast fortune that was at the heart of problems in this sibling-versus-sibling, two-generation soap saga. Larry Hagman, Patrick Duffy, Linda Gray, Victoria Principal, and Barbara Bel Geddes were among the principal cast members of this series, which debuted on April 2, 1978, and ran until May of 1991. It was one of the most popular shows in the history of the medium.

The Ewings lived at the Southfork Ranch, which is located fifteen miles from the Dallas city limits in suburban Parker County. The ranch's rainbow-gated entrance and impressive, multi-columned white mansion are recognized around the world. So many people came looking for it, soon after the show began, that they clogged the two-lane road leading to it.

It became an almost overnight trouble spot for locals, and its real owner, J. R. Duncan, got so irked with people looking into his windows that he opted to sell his forty-one–acre spread to the Trippet Company. This corporate owner, seeking to profit from the tourist trade, paved pastures into parking lots and constructed a half-million-dollar convention center. The mansion was offered for guest rentals at a weeknight rate of $2,500 and $3,000 for weekend nights. The new corporate owners opened gift and souvenir shops and began operating a $4.00 tour of the grounds (a dollar extra for a stagecoach tour). The *Dallas* Museum was opened in 1988. Its exhibits include J.R.'s hat and boots; the gown Sue Ellen wore to the Cattle Barons' Ball; Jock's last will and testament; the script for the show's two-hour pilot; and taped interviews with cast members.

Southfork's tourist business boomed throughout the 1980s. More than 400,000 people a year, from eighty-six different countries, came to this lush stretch of TV Land. The end-of-the-decade's slide into economic recession, however, and the show's cancellation in 1990, eventually prompted the Trippet Company to sell the ranch. It became, once again, the property of J. R. Duncan. He closed it down for a year and a half and spent a quarter of a million dollars on improvements. Reopened in 1992, Southfork now boasts a Visitor's Center, an art gallery, and a shopping complex in addition to its other attractions.

## Getting in Touch

The Southfork Ranch's management advises those who'd like to see the Ewing spread call them at (214)442-6531. They'll make reservations, quote tour prices, and give detailed directions on how to reach the ranch from Dallas. They're open from 9 A.M. until 6 P.M., seven days a week.

Seven Brides for
Seven Brothers

Washington

Oregon
Trail

Oregon

Buckskin

My
Friend
Flicka

Montana

North
Dakota

The
Dakotas

Father
Murphy

Idaho

The
Monroes

South
Dakota

Man
Without
a Gun

The
Ponderosa

Wyoming

Have Gun,
Will Travel

Nevada

Laramie

Nebraska

Barbary
Coast

Big Valley

Utah

Fort Baxter

Death Valley

Fort Roswell

California

Colorado

Dodge
City

Kansas

Zorro

Hotel de
Paree

Roy
Rogers

The Rifleman
(North Fork)

Cimmaron
Strip

Arizona

McCloud
(Taos)

Oklahoma

Death
Valley Days

Fort
Apache

New Mexico

The
Outlaws

Hec
Ramsey

Bret Maverick
(Sweetwater)

Old
Tucson

Santa Fe
Trail
(Santa Fe)

Rawhide
(Abilene)

Gunslinger

Tombstone

The Lone
Ranger

Texas

Laredo

N

W · E

S

# TV LAND'S
# WILD
# WEST

The mythical Gloomy River cuts through the Wild West. Promontories range from Lost Mountain to a chain of generic Boot Hills. Among the most forlorn of its wildernesses are the Badlands, Superstition Prairie, and Death Valley. Towns such as Epitaph, Tombstone, and Deadwood signify some kind of spiritual as well as geographic end of the road.

The Oregon, the Chisholm, and the Santa Fe trails meander across the region. There is always some kind of traffic headed west: wagon trains, iron horses, stagecoaches, the Pony Express, buckboards, Indian war parties, cavalry brigades, bands of outlaws on the run, sheriffs' posses in pursuit, cattle drives, buffalo stampedes. There are mesas, plateaus, dry washes, mountain passes, salt flats, and desert basins to pass through. There always seems to be some overwhelming obstacle in the way: a gully or a gulch; a caved-in mine shaft; an almost-impossible-to-escape-from box canyon.

The titles of several cowboy series denoted just where in the

Wild West they took place: *Laramie, Cimmaron Strip, Laredo, Oregon Trail, Tales of the Texas Rangers, Tombstone Territory.* Some titles gave indication of local topography: *The Big Valley, Death Valley Days, The Barbary Coast, High Chaparral.*

Fashion statements, made by some of the region's leading heroes, give hints of the region's cultural identity. The color scheme of good guys wearing white hats and bad guys wearing black hats was elaborated on by the likes of, for example, *Hopalong Cassidy.*

Chuck Connors *(left)* gave up playing baseball in the Los Angeles Dodgers organization and went on to become Lucas McCain — The Rifleman. When he wasn't busy shooting up the Wild West (he was on the Good Guys In The White Hats team, of course), The Rifleman was said to ranch a spread near North Fork, New Mexico. He was a single parent—a skinnier and taller and younger and poorer Ben Cartwright. Also unlike Ben, he had but one son. Johnny Crawford played Mark McCain, only child and solitary ranch hand. *Courtesy of Four Star Films.*

Cassidy turned basic black and white into haute couture by dressing in all white while riding Topper, his black horse. *The Lone Ranger*, too, wore all white while riding Silver, his white stallion.

Basic black was the choice of Adam Cartwright (*Bonanza*) as well as of Paladin (*Have Gun, Will Travel*)—a man who never left his rooms in San Francisco's St. Francis Hotel without a suitcase filled with more black ensembles to wear during his travels. *Zorro*, who lived in Monterey, California, was the most resplendent hero of all. His all-black outfit, from boots to hat, included a black cape. *Zorro* not only had a white but a black horse, too, at his disposal.

It wasn't just essential wardrobe items, but sometimes accessories (like the dazzling gun belt holding the silver bullets used by the *Lone Ranger*), that functioned as icons symbolizing the Wild West. *Maverick* was easily known by the flashy vests he wore. Paladin's business card provided immediate identification, and the hallmark of *Bat Masterson* was the cane he carried, which held a concealed knife blade at its tip.

Certain, unsolved mysteries await anyone who ventures through this region. Did, for example, Ben Cartwright's three, pre-*Bonanza* wives (each of whom bore him a son) really die the way he told the boys they had? Did the cattle drive from North Texas to Sedalia, Kansas (as seen on *Rawhide*), last for seven years without reaching its destination? Were any of the descendants of the men of Fort Courage's *F Troop* among those funny soldiers known as *Hogan's Heroes*? Searching for the answers to these and other questions is all part of the quest for those seeking out the shoot 'em up world of TV Land's Wild West. . . .

*Opposite page, right:* James Garner was Maverick, a man who roamed from town to town in the Wild West, always looking for a card game with less than talented gamblers but with a pot rich enough for his liking. This series had several incarnations; the last one (*Bret Maverick*) showed him settling down in Sweetwater, Arizona. Maverick put down roots there after winning the town's Red Ox Saloon as well as the nearby Lazy Ace Ranch in a poker game. *Courtesy of ABC-TV.*

# THE RANCHES OF THE WILD WEST

Just as a man's home is his castle, a cowboy's ranch was his kingdom. Many of this region's ranches were as big as some feudal kingdoms, in some cases even bigger. The 500,000 acre Garret Ranch, outside of Santa Fe, New Mexico, was one of the largest. It was the setting for the aptly titled *Empire*, which ran for thirty-two episodes between 1962 and 1964. Ryan O'Neal played the son of the ranch's owner and Charles Bronson was cast as a ranch hand.

The Lancer Ranch (*Lancer*, 1970–71) was a spread of 100,000 acres in California's San Joaquin Valley. This series was created by David Dortort, who was also responsible for *Bonanza* and *High Chaparral*. The San Joaquin was also *The Big Valley* where, just outside of Stockton, the Barkley Ranch spread for some 30,000 acres. Victoria Barkley (played by Barbara Stanwyck) oversaw operation of the ranch—which included a mine, a vineyard, and an orange grove—with the help of her children. Two of her offspring were later to become multimillion-dollar players: Lee Majors, *The Six Million Dollar Man*, and Linda Evans, who became Krystle Carrington of *Dynasty*. *The Big Valley* ran from 1965 to 1969.

Wyoming was prime-time ranch territory. The ranches around *Laramie* (1959–63) were thriving in the 1880s. The Shiloh Ranch, in Medicine Bow, was the setting for both *The Virginian* (1962–70) and *The Men from Shiloh* (1970–71). The Goose Bay Ranch, in Coulee Springs, was where *My Friend Flicka* was stabled for the 1956–57 TV season. (Flicka is Swedish for *little girl*.) The

Flying Crown Ranch, near Grover City, Arizona, featured a runway where *Sky King* (1951–56) made weekly takeoffs and landings.

Notable ranches, for which no specific geographic location was given, include the Bar Twenty Ranch (*Hopalong Cassidy*), the Broken Wheel Ranch (*Fury*, 1956–66), and the Flying A Ranch of *The Gene Autry Show* (1950–56).

# THE LONE RANGER

*The Lone Ranger* was one of the very first TV series, debuting on September 15, 1949, with Clayton Moore as John Reid—the man in the mask. The show already had, however, a national reputation; it had played on radio since 1933. It was a big hit from the start, with its inevitable ride "into the sunset" not coming until the fall of 1957.

When he first rode into TV Land he wasn't really "lone"; he was part of a posse of six rangers, one of whom was his brother. They all rode into an ambush, executed by Butch Cavendish's Hole-in-the-Wall Gang, as they entered Bryant's Gap Canyon in Texas.

John Reid was the only survivor, and he wouldn't have made it without being rescued by a Powatomie Indian named Tonto. Tonto dug six graves and buried the five men. The sixth grave was meant to fool Butch and his boys into thinking the ambush had been a total success. Tonto also made his buddy a mask, using Reid's dead brother's vest for material.

From bloody Bryant's Gap Canyon, the two of them roamed across TV Land's Wild West in search of villainy. They never took any money for their work. Instead, the Lone Ranger and Tonto would occasionally visit a secret silver mine that Reid and his brother had discovered together. It's where his silver bullets came from, too.

For a fellow whose job entitled him to legal authority only on a territorial basis, the Lone Ranger really got around. He may have been a Texas Ranger, but he ranks as one of the most uniquely peripatetic of heroes in all of TV Land. While Bryant's Gap Canyon is where he first made history, there are Lone Ranger landmarks found in both Arizona and California.

# The Lone Ranger's Five Location-Shoot Landmarks

## Bronson Canyon

The original opening of *The Lone Ranger* was shot in this canyon, which rises above Hollywood, California.

## Corriganville

Most of *The Lone Ranger*'s 221 episodes were shot at this movie ranch in the Simi Valley, close to Los Angeles.

## Vasquez Rocks

Many Westerns, including scenes of *The Lone Ranger*, were shot here. This wild, boulder-strewn area is in the Santa Clarita Valley, near Los Angeles.

## Old Tucson

*The Lone Ranger* rode the range here looking for the Lost City of Gold.

## Iverson Movie Ranch

This old movie ranch, which is in the Chatsworth area of Los Angeles's San Fernando Valley, is the location of Lone Ranger Rock . . . the place where Silver always rears up on his hind legs.

These two fellows were on a constant lookout for trouble. Wearing a mask never seemed to prevent the Lone Ranger from noticing the slightest tracks made by man or beast. Likewise, Tonto's headband was never tight enough to prevent the circulation of blood to his brain. *Courtesy of the Wrather Corp.*

# Tonto Tidbits

Jay Silverheels, who played Tonto, wasn't really a member of the Powatomie tribe; he was a Mohawk Indian. He was born on the Six Nations Reservation in Ontario, Canada. He had an affinity for the word *scout*. Not only was it the name of his horse, but *kemo sabe* (which is what Tonto called John Reid) means "trusted scout."

# WILD WEST TV LAND GEOGRAPHIA

## A Place in the Sun

Being the lowest and hottest place in the whole continent, Death Valley ought to qualify as the most inhospitable terrain to be found in TV Land. But such is not the case. This stretch of scorching California high desert nourished the careers of Stanley Andrews, Ronald Reagan, Robert Taylor, and Dale Robertson, who succeeded each other as the hosts of *Death Valley Days* over the eighteen years (1953–70) that this Western ran on television. Cowboy desperados, however, weren't the only people to find haven here.

## A Place in the Sun II

Due to Death Valley's reputation as being a kind of "hell on earth," Gomez and Morticia Addams (*The Addams Family*) chose it as their honeymoon destination.

## Rocks of the Ages

The twenty-million-year-old Vasquez Rocks, which are in the Santa Clarita Valley near Los Angeles, have been seen in myriad films. They became part of TV Land when *The Lone Ranger* and *The Cisco Kid* first rode through this area in the 1950s. The boys from *Bonanza* and the Barkleys of *The Big Valley* followed in the

Roy and Dale have their museum in Victorville, California, a high desert town where the living legend coexists with his stuffed horse and dog.
*Courtesy of Roy Rogers Productions.*

1960s. Vasquez Rocks has also served as the setting for episodes of *Battlestar Galactica* and *Murder, She Wrote*. Its most important role was in *Star Trek*, in which it served as Mr. Spock's home planet of Vulcan.

# The Roy Rogers and Dale Evans Museum

Hundreds of mementos from this TV cowboy/cowgirl couple's past are on display in their Victorville, California, museum. The most popular attractions are the preserved animals: Roy's horse, Trigger; Dale's horse, Buttermilk; and their dog, Bullet. The museum is at 15650 Seneca Road in Victorville, California. It's open daily from 9 A.M. until 5 P.M.

Two of the many types of collectibles featured at the Roy Rogers and Dale Evans Museum include the lithographed Thermos tin lunchbox kit and the official Roy Rogers and Trigger holster outfit in the original box. *Courtesy of Robert Heide and John Gilman* Box-Office Buckaroos *Collection.*

# Faux Ancient Ruins

Corriganville is TV Land's Pompeii: a once-thriving center of commerce and art, which the forces of time and natural cataclysm combined to destroy. Corriganville was the creation of B-movie actor Crash Corrigan who, after buying a few thousand Southern California acres in 1937, developed his holdings into an extremely successful film location for Hollywood Westerns. It was opened to the public in 1949 as a Wild West amusement park and drew some 20,000 people on weekends. It became a part of TV Land in the 1950s, when its terrain of dusty hillsides, chaparral, groves of trees, and impressive rock formations attracted the attention of producers. Episodes of both *Gunsmoke* and *Have Gun, Will Travel* were shot here. Corriganville was also where *Rin Tin Tin* used to sniff the air for the scent of danger and where the Lone Ranger's mighty stallion Silver's hooves once thundered.

Bob Hope bought the land in 1965 and shut it down to the public a year later. The sets, which included the *Rin Tin Tin* show's Fort Apache, went up in flames in 1970 and again in 1979. Today, its ruins may be seen up by the Santa Susanna Pass, at the far eastern end of the Simi Valley, close to the Los Angeles/Ventura county line.

**LAKE TAHOE** *Ben Cartwright's*
## Ponderosa Ranch

**Home of "Bonanza"**
Incline Village, Nevada, USA

On the North Shore of
Beautiful Lake Tahoe

# The Ponderosa

*Bonanza* painted a picture of the Wild West as more than merely an arena for bullets to fly, cattle to cross, and the plundering of riches from the earth . . . though, surely, all these things happened during the course of the show. More significantly, the show sometimes managed to incorporate such historical figures as writers Charles Dickens and Mark Twain, actor Edwin Booth, and the pirate Jean Lafitte in its storylines.

The four principal characters, and the actors who played them, were as dynamic as the series' rugged setting. Lorne Greene was Ben Cartwright, a man who raised three sons on his own. Pernell Roberts played the eldest son, Adam.

THE LIVING LEGEND OF BONANZA...
PONDEROSA RANCH
STORY

FULL COLOR POSTCARDS INSIDE

$169

Dan Blocker was Hoss. Michael Landon (who went on to both mastermind and star in *Little House on the Prairie* and *Highway to Heaven*) played the youngest son, Little Joe Cartwright.

*Bonanza* ran from September of 1959 to January of 1973, but the fact that the series left the prime-time network airwaves more than two decades ago hasn't diminished the drawing power of the Cartwright's Ponderosa Ranch. An average of 250,000 people from all over the world make a pilgrimage to this TV Land shrine every year. *Bonanza* finished in the top-ten list of the most popular of series for nine years and ranked as number one for three years in a row. It was translated into twelve different languages and seen in eighty-six nations where an estimated half a billion people became familiar with the Cartwright name. Widely rerun in syndication, the show spawned a 1987 TV movie and then a new series—*Bonanza: The Next Generation.*

## The Ponderosa History According to Television

It was back in the 1850s when Ben Cartwright, after having completed his tour of duty in the merchant marine, left his native New England and journeyed West. Intent on reaching California, where he hoped to have his own bit of paradise, Ben's odyssey came to an unexpected end when he reached the Nevada shoreline of Lake Tahoe and decided this was the place for him to make history.

The year was 1859. Silver was being mined in the Truckee River Valley. Ben became a land owner and, during the years that followed, developed holdings until the Ponderosa spread across some 3,000 square miles of the Sierra Nevada. It was a cowboy empire of wilderness and range without rival.

# About the Map

Watching the opening of *Bonanza* was a lesson in speed map-reading. The TV screen would fill with the Ponderosa map, and flames erupted and began to burn inward from its edges. Viewers had about four seconds to spot Reno, Carson City, and Virginia City before the whole thing went up in smoke.

The map could also be seen whenever Ben Cartwright was shown at work in his home office. It hung on the wall just behind his desk. If you were particularly sharp-eyed you had a chance, every now and then, to take a passing glance at it and perhaps note the Ponderosa's geographic proximity to Lake Tahoe, the smaller Washoe Lake, and the nearby Truckee River.

# The Story Behind the Ranch

The Ponderosa became something more than just a place that existed in creator David Dortort's imagination when NBC decided, soon after the show's inception, to send cast and crew to the Tahoe region for some exterior location shoots. The show's aura of authenticity was dramatically increased later on when the Cartwright's imposing, redwood-planked manse was built. Some interior shoots were transferred from a Culver City TV studio to the ranch location.

Hollywood's invasion of this rural Nevada alpine region did not take place without attracting a good bit of notice. At first it was the curious local citizens who, attracted by the bright lights, found their way to where the cameras were capturing the Cartwrights on film. The locals were followed in increasing numbers, and from ever more distant originations, as the show gained in popularity by bonafide *Bonanza* fans.

The idea that the Ponderosa had the potential to be a place that the public would pay to see was hatched by area residents Bill and

Joyce Andersen in 1967. It became a kind of *Field of Dreams* obsession. Bill, who had worked there as an equipment contractor, took on the highly improbable task of enlisting backers and getting the cooperation of NBC. TV myth became a tourist reality when the Ponderosa was officially dedicated on June 13, 1968. The event was treated as if it was of significant historical importance. As made obvious by the imposing bronze plaque it issued, the state of Nevada took the whole thing so seriously it made no differentiation between the illusory TV Land and the actual United States of America.

The plaque, which bears the names of then Governor Paul Laxalt, NBC executive vice president Thomas Sarnoff, show creator David Dortort, and the men who played the Cartwright clan, reads:

> Welcome to the Ponderosa
> This house honors the pioneer spirit of the Sierra Nevada: the courage, resourcefulness, and sense of destiny possessed by the men and women who crossed the prairies, forced the mountains, settled the valleys, and forever linked the distant shores of a sprawling young nation.

# Going on Tour

If you're one of those legion of fans who just might want to walk in Little Joe's footsteps and behold the baronial splendor that Ben and his three boys lived in, then you must add the Ponderosa Ranch to your list of must-see destinations. The Ponderosa tour begins at the ranch's parking lot, where visitors board motorized hay wagons for the short ride up the mountain. The wagons pass scattered hunks of rusted farm equipment and unload their pas-

Go to the Ponderosa and you'll meet Hopsing — man of wax and cook to cowboy blue bloods.
*Courtesy of Robin Keats.*

Long before there were savings and loans, there were places such as the Liberty Bank, where hard-earned money had a good chance of being stolen.
*Courtesy of Robin Keats.*

sengers at a picnic area. Ranch hands serve up the Hay Wagon Breakfast of Ben's Scrambled Eggs, Hopsing's Sausage, flapjacks, juice, and coffee for $2.00. After breakfast, tour guides lead everyone for a short uphill walk to the house and barn. Everyone is shepherded into the barn for a showing of a brief videotaped introduction to the Ponderosa and then led to the house itself.

The atmosphere is decidedly surreal once you get beyond the front door. The first sight to behold is rather startling. There before you stands the waxen facsimile of Hopsing, the Chinese cook. He's standing behind a kitchen counter, looking right at you and holding a meat cleaver in his raised right hand! His kitchen, however, is the real thing, complete with antique stove, table, cooking utensils, and dinnerware. Tour groups are led past the kitchen and into the finely furnished dining room. The table is set as if the Cartwrights are expected to arrive for dinner at any second. The living room, with its huge fireplace and stuffed chairs, would be an appropriate setting for a nineteenth-century episode of *Lifestyles of the Rich and Famous*.

According to the show, Ben decked out the house with furniture he had collected during his sailing days from the world's most exotic ports. No room exemplifies this as much as the study. The magnificent desk and ornate cabinetry attest that Ben was really worth some bucks. Tour guides direct attention to the staircase that ascends from the living room. The house was built not by traditional builders but by TV set designers. No scenes were ever written for the bedrooms, so the staircase leads to nowhere. There are, however, a couple of hidden chambers in the house. They were constructed to hold the camera crews out of view while film was rolling. Once the guides point this out, they lead their groups out the back door. The guided portion of the tour is over. Visitors are left to wander on to the Western town, a few hundred yards distant, at their own pace.

# What's Going on in Town

The collection of brightly painted real and mock buildings is referred to, in Ponderosa literature, as "the Western town." That's it. They don't dare call it Virginia City—the place where the *Bonanza* cowboys did their drinking, gambling, banking, and bordelloing—because the real and carefully restored Virginia City is but a twenty-minute drive from the ranch.

There is life in this ersatz environment, but it won't always be found where you might expect it. The Liberty Bank, the Bath House, and the Dentist's Clinic are all false-front structures. Sheriff Coffee's Office, with his name printed in golden letters on the glass-paned door, looks real, but there's nothing behind the door.

The General Store is a cavernous emporium that sells an utterly overwhelming variety of Ponderosa-stamped cowboy kitsch. There's Ponderosa whiskey, shot glasses, cigars, pencil erasers, ski jackets, toy rifles, maps, ties, hats, jackets, sweatshirts, sun visors, sculptures, paintings, postcards, wallets—bric-a-brac ad infinitum.

You can rent period costumes and have your picture taken while you're dressed in Sunday-go-to-meeting clothes at the Old Time Photo Studio. While playing dress-up in front of the camera is popular with parent-types, kiddies will find the unsophisticated challenges of Hoss's Mystery Mine and the Shooting Gallery more to their liking. Kids will probably also want to visit the Pet-

After Adam took off, Ben had to rely on his two younger sons — Hoss and Little Joe. They, unlike their rebellious brother, stayed home with Pa for the entire run of the series.    *Courtesy of NBC-TV.*

ting Zoo, a modest menagerie of baby goats, lambs, calves, and chicks. The Ponderosa also offers free pony rides and mock gunfights, too. The Western Memorabilia Museum is jammed with artifacts that were once essential to life on the range: harnesses and saddles, pistols and rifles, knives, branding irons, and other assorted cowboy gear. There's also the Antique Farm and Ranch Equipment Display, and the truly charming 1870 Church of the Ponderosa, which is nearly as big an attraction as the Cartwright house.

Weddings are scheduled on an almost daily basis and the bookings are made weeks, sometimes months, in advance. One hundred and fifty dollars is the package price for Ponderosa-style nuptials, with the church rental, the minister's fee, a wedding photo, and limousine ride to and from the parking lot all included.

## Food and Drink

Though probably not up to the culinary standards of Hopsing, the Ponderosa pays tribute to the legendary appetite of Hoss Cartwright with each serving of the Hoss-burger Luncheon. This meal includes a "hearty Hoss-burger with trimmings," ranch beans, and coffee or a soft drink. Adults can fill their bellies for $10.50, kids five to eleven are charged $8.50, and tykes under five face a $4.00 tab. Thirsty folks are advised to head for the Silver Dollar Saloon, which serves up most everything from cola to Kahlua. Every drink is poured into a free, take-home Ponderosa souvenir tin cup. If you want dessert, be prepared to wait on line. The Old Time Ice Cream Parlor is the only place in town that offers it.

## Getting There

The Ponderosa, at Incline Village, is a forty-mile drive on Interstate 112 from the gateway city of Reno. It's a beautiful ride up to the crestline of the Sierra Nevada Mountains and then down to the shores of spectacular Lake Tahoe. The Interstate terminates at the road that circles the lake. Bear left, which will have you heading east, and drive along the shoreline for three miles. Turn left at the large sign that marks the entrance to the ranch at 100 Ponderosa Ranch Road.

Open seven days a week, from May through October, the ranch hours are from 9:30 A.M. until 5 P.M. The guided tours usually run about three hours and the parking is always free. The price is $7.50 for adults and kids, from the ages of five to eleven, are charged $5.50.

# Tombstone Territory

Founded in 1879, home to over 10,000 people at its peak, site of the O.K. Corral and the place where Wyatt Earp's twin .45 Buntline Specials tried to instill some degree of law and order, Tombstone, Arizona, rivals Dodge City, Kansas, for supremacy in TV Land's Wild West. Though only some 1,200 people now live here, Tombstone manages to attract approximately 100,000 visitors on an annual basis.

Wild West aficionados will truly appreciate the authentic ambiance of this once-upon-a-time frontier community. There are those who'll especially enjoy reading the inscriptions on the grave-markers of Boothill Cemetery and others who'll seek and find their pleasures in drink over at the Crystal Palace, where Wyatt Earp used to run an ongoing poker game. Of course, no one can

*Wyatt Earp.* Hugh O'Brian played the lawman who shot it out with the bad guys at the O.K. Corral in Tombstone, Arizona. Today, he's the author's next-door neighbor. *Courtesy of Hugh O'Brian.*

This is historic Dodge City, Kansas, as it actually looked in the 1870s.
*Courtesy of Boot Hill Museum, Inc., Dodge City, Kansas.*

avoid missing the regularly staged reenactments of the infamous Gunfight at the O.K. Corral.

Tombstone enlisted in the Mainstreet Program, run by the National Trust for Historic Preservation, in 1991. Restoration work along Allen Street, in the core of the historic district, has given the area much the same look it had when Wyatt, Virgil, and Morgan Earp (plus their pal Doc Holliday) shot it out with the Clanton Gang at the O.K. in 1881.

## Tombstone's Place in TV Land

Tombstone occupies a unique position in the annals of TV Land because it was showcased on the tube over the course of four television seasons by two different TV series. *Tombstone Territory,* which ran from September of 1957 to September of 1958 (and, again, from March of 1959 through September of that year), focused on the exploits of Sheriff Clay Hollister. *The Life and Legend of Wyatt Earp* featured the title's namesake legend and ran from 1955 through 1961. Earp's show originally placed him in Dodge City: he was that town's marshall from 1955 through 1959, concurrent with the tour of duty made by Marshall Matt Dillon of *Gunsmoke*. The two of them never managed to meet during their four years together in the same town, though it wasn't because Dodge City was so big that it kept them from crossing each other's paths. They avoided what would seem to have been an inevitable confrontation only because the two shows ran on different networks!

**Tombstone's Civic Motto:** *"The town too tough to die."*

*"No question—the quirkiness of the town does attract a goofball element . . . people out there who never stopped playing cowboys and Indians."*
—Hollis Cook, manager of the Tombstone
Courthouse State Historic Park

# Dodge City

The most witnessed duel ever to have taken place in TV Land is the one seen in the opening of *Gunsmoke*—an event seen once a week, from the 1950s to the 1970s on TV's longest running Western. Even though *Gunsmoke* (which starred James Arness as Marshall Dillon, Amanda Blake as Miss Kitty, and Milburn Stone as Doc) departed from the prime-time airwaves in 1975, this shootout continues to take place four times daily, from Memorial Day to Labor Day, year after year. No place does more than Dodge City to demonstrate the part it plays in the story of TV Land.

Miss Kitty and her boys (the Marshall, Quint, Doc, and Festus) on the studio mock-up of Dodge City's Front Street.  *Courtesy of CBS-TV.*

Dodge City is situated on the banks of the Arkansas River in western Kansas. It was, at the time of its founding, the end point of the Chisholm and the Western trails. Each ran for about 1,000 miles and both were used by cattlemen who drove their herds over them from Texas to the rail-shipping center that Dodge City became after the end of the Civil War.

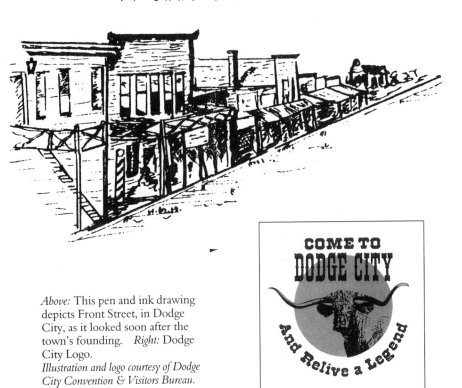

*Above:* This pen and ink drawing depicts Front Street, in Dodge City, as it looked soon after the town's founding. *Right:* Dodge City Logo.
*Illustration and logo courtesy of Dodge City Convention & Visitors Bureau.*

Saddle-sore cowboys, after a four-month drive, exchanged cows for cash when they got to town. Waiting to take their money were plenty of saloons, poker parlors, and Wild West hookers. It took months, not years, for Dodge City to garner the reputation of being "the Queen of the cow towns," "the toughest town on the map," "the wickedest little city in America," and "the bilious Babylon of the frontier."

Founded in 1872, Dodge City quickly grew into a community of about 1,000 people within five years. In 1877, there were sixteen saloons, two dance halls, and at least forty-seven prostitutes doing business in Dodge City. Among the great and the vainglorious who lived, worked, and/or broke the law here were Wyatt Earp, Bat Masterson, Wild Bill Hickok, Doc Holliday, Johnny Ringo, Billy the Kid, and Belle Starr.

## Front Street Leads Back to Gunsmoking Glory Days

Prompted by the popularity of *Gunsmoke*, Dodge City embarked on an extensive re-creation of its most historic district, which runs along Front Street, in the 1950s. Every year, 100,000 visitors (over 20,000 from foreign countries during 1993 alone) come here to tour an area that includes a museum, the Boot Hill Cemetery, Front Street's historic shops, stores, saloons, and office buildings, and several other nearby structures.

The Boot Hill Museum offers exhibits and interpretative programs that detail the lives of the cattle and sheep ranchers, the buffalo hunters, the famous lawmen and infamous outlaws, and the Plains Indians. There are collections of firearms, farm equipment, musical and gambling machines, period furniture, tribal artifacts, and even a vintage mortuary display of caskets and funeral shrouds in this "village museum" complex.

The Boot Hill Cemetery is a much-reduced copy of the original boneyard. Thirty bodies were exhumed when it was officially closed in 1879. Today, there are several mock graves, situated in the shade offered by a hanging tree, for tourists to visit. There's also one fresh, undesignated hole in the ground suitable as a setting for morbid picture-taking.

Front Street is lined by several saloons, a restaurant, a general store, a dry goods store, a cigar store, a drugstore, a hardware store, a doctor's office, a newspaper office, a barber, a gunsmith, and a blacksmith shop. Mock gunfights and Medicine Shows are staged along the street throughout the summer season.

The Long Branch Saloon is still the liveliest place in town. Miss

Reconstruction has transformed Front Street into the tourist attraction it is today.    *Courtesy of Dodge City Convention & Visitors Bureau.*

Kitty and her Cancan Dancers present a nightly variety show on summer evenings. Look for old Doc Adams, long retired from the bullet-wound-mending business, to be accompanying Miss Kitty on the saloon's piano.

## Other Destinations in and Around Dodge City

The Fort Dodge Jail
The Hardesty House
The Beeson Gallery
The One-Room School
The Santa Fe Trail Tracks
The Famous Gunfighter's Wax Museum

## "If You Go" Info

Admission to Front Street and Boot Hill is $3.75. For detailed material concerning accommodations, dining, and travel services write to: Dodge City Chamber of Commerce, P.O. Box 939, Dodge City, Kansas 67801.

*High Chaparral.* According to the show's creators, the Cannon family ranch was a cattleman's empire (circa 1870s), located in the heart of Apache Territory. Naturally, Apache chief Cochise didn't feel very neighborly toward the ranchers who came to build fences and raise cows for slaughter on his turf. While Cochise and the conditions he had to deal with were real, the ranch, pictured above and opposite, is just a stop on the tour through Old Tucson Studios.
*Courtesy of NBC-TV.*

# Old Tucson

No television series ever bore the name or even a variation of the name Tucson, but its prominent place in TV Land is undeniable. It got its start in 1939, when Columbia Pictures erected a replica of what Tucson looked like in the 1860s. This set, located a dozen miles from the modern city, was used only for film making until 1957, when TV's Lone Ranger came riding through, looking for the Lost City of Gold.

Since that time, it developed into the busiest place in TV's Wild West, perhaps in all of TV Land. *Wagon Train* arrived in 1959, and Paladin (of *Have Gun, Will Travel*) came on business in 1962. Following him were the Cartwrights, Marshall Dillon, *The New Mavericks, The Sacketts, Father Murphy,* and *The Young Riders.* Some stayed just for an episode or two; others for entire seasons. In addition to all the cowboys, Old Tucson has also been a romping

ground for *Petrocelli*, *Hart to Hart*, and *Webster*. It added the role of theme park to its movie and TV functions in 1960 and grew to be the biggest privately operated tourist attraction in all of Arizona. Visitors, should they happen to carefully time their trips here, can watch shows in production inside the soundstages or at such Old Tucson locations as High Chaparral/Fort Reunion, Mescal, and the Mexican Plaza and Mission. Front Street is filled with the sounds of Sapphire Sue's Musical Revue, performed daily at the Red Dog Saloon. Mock gunfights, stunt demonstrations, and magic acts keep both Front and Kansas streets filled with action. More tricks and illusions take place indoors at the Soundstage's Royal Oak Saloon. There are usually four different live shows—illusions, musicals, drama, and even vaudeville—running in the Soundstage. The documentary *Hollywood in the Desert* (a fifteen-minute video about the whole place) plays every half hour in the Arizona Theater.

## Stepping Out to Eat...

The restaurants "in town" include the Iron Door Cafe, the Coyote Cafe, and Big Jake's BBQ. Sugar fixes are available at The Golden Nugget Old Fashioned Ice Cream Parlor and Ma Shelton's Bakery.

## Stepping Out to Shop...

Ten specialty shops take all four major credit cards. There are stores selling Indian jewelry and rugs, movie memorabilia, clothes, and boots. They, along with the drugstore, a print shop, and an art gallery, form the downtown business core of Old Tucson.

## Stepping Back in Time...

Old Tucson packs a lot of historical reminders behind its Old West wooden gates. They include the displays and collections at the Boardwalk Hall of Fame, the Gun Museum, the Kachina Museum, and the Firehouse Museum. There are also reproductions of a nineteenth-century Assay Office and an Apothecary and an exhibit at the Red Dog Hotel.

## Stepping Off After the Kiddies...

Old Tucson is a town without pity for the TV Land purist. In addition to big-time commercialism, there's also a powerful diversion offered (to kids) by Silverlake Park. Opened in 1977, it's got an old-time carousel; a Stutz-Bearcat race car ride; a narrow-gauge railroad ride; the kid-powered Iron Pony ride; and the Rio Bravo mini-canoe water-trough ride. Juveniles and/or their elders who might be nauseated by such experiences can opt to pan for gold, play old-time games of skill as well as those in a video arcade; descend into a mine, take off in a stagecoach or get back to nature for a little while at Grandpa's Petting Zoo.

## Going to Town...

Old Tucson is open every day, all year, from 9 A.M. to 9 P.M. Admission is modestly priced for adults and for kids, and is reduced for the after-five crowd. Kids under three enter free. Call (602)883-0100 for more information.

Twin Peaks

Northern
Exposure

Washington

Hello, Larry
(Portland)

Oregon

N
W ✦ E
S

(San Francisco)
Streets of San
Francisco
Ironside
Full House
My Sister Sam

Nevada

(Sacramento)
Eight Is Enough

Donny and
Marie

Mork and
Mindy
(Boulder)
Dynasty
(Denver)

Utah

Colorado

Vegas
(Las Vegas)

California Camp
Henderson
Gomer Pyle,
U.S.M.C.

Bedrock

Sky King

(San Diego)
Simon and
Simon

Arizona

New Mexico

(Los Angeles)
Family
Gidget
Marcus Welby, M.D.
Quincy
The Beverly Hillbillies
Beverly Hills 90210
77 Sunset Strip
Melrose Place
L.A. Law
Ozzie and Harriet
My Three Sons
Rocky and Bullwinkle
TV Land Babylon
Tombs of TV Land

Alice
(Phoenix)

Petrocelli
(San Remo)

Hey, Dude
(Tucson)

# WESTERN
# TV
# LAND

The West of the modern era (post-cowboy times) remained the Promised Land for those seeking a better life in the peaceful, civilized territory that had been the once-upon-a-time frontier. People came here from everywhere. From Norway came the Hansens of *Mama* (1949–57). Mama Marta and Papa Lars moved into a house in San Francisco and raised three Americanized children there. *The Real McCoys* left West Virginia for Southern California's San Fernando Valley in 1959. *The Beverly Hillbillies* took leave of the Ozark Mountains and re-established themselves in Beverly Hills in 1962. *My Favorite Martian* left his home planet and arrived in Los Angeles on a Sunday night in 1963. *My Three Sons* relocated from generic Hillsdale to North Hollywood when Steve Douglas was given a job transfer to one of the region's defense plants.

After losing his job at WJM-TV in Minneapolis, *Lou Grant* came West in 1977 and found work as the city editor of the *Los Angeles Tribune*. And after *Laverne and Shirley* lost their jobs in a

In *77 Sunset Strip,* Efrem Zimbalist, Jr., played Stu Bailey, a private investigator. His detective agency had one of the hippest addresses in all of TV land...right next to Dino's nightclub on L.A.'s glamorous Sunset Boulevard. *Courtesy of ABC-TV.*

Milwaukee brewery, they, too, came west to Los Angeles in 1980, finding employment in a department store.

All these characters were to live out variations on *The Life of Riley* (1949–50; 1953–58). Chester A. Riley had a really decent life, considering his intelligence. Like Ralph Kramden, he was a quintessential blue-collar worker of the fifties. Unlike Kramden, however, Riley owned his own home. It was in a decent Los Angeles neighborhood, at 1313 Blue View Terrace, right next door to pals Jim Gillis and his wife, Honeybee—the Ed and Trixie Norton of the West.

Riley (like Steve Douglas) worked in the region's aerospace industry. He was a riveter by trade and was able to afford, on his $110-a-week salary, not only a wife but two children and a dog. The East meets West, Kramden/Riley connection is also marked by the casting history involved with *The Life of Riley* and *The Honeymooners*. Though William Bendix had been the star of *Riley* when it was a radio series, it was Jackie Gleason who was chosen to portray Chester Riley when the TV version began airing on October 4, 1949. It ran for twenty-six weeks and was canceled. When it was revived in January of 1953, Bendix was back in the title role. This time, the show was a success and ran until August of 1958. Gleason went on to become Kramden and, perhaps, chose to forget (in his tiny two-room apartment) that life in the West was easier than it was in Brooklyn...just as it was apparently easier than in West Virginia or the Ozarks or Milwaukee, too, though certainly, judging by

As Perry Mason, Raymond Burr lived his life in a court room. As Ironsides, he called San Francisco home.
*Courtesy of Viacom.*

Uncle Martin's attitude, not better than life on Mars. While the Western region sprawls over eleven states—from the Canadian border to Mexico and from the Rocky Mountains to the Pacific Ocean—its TV Land population is heavily concentrated in the Southern California area. This area subdivides into such major sections as the beach, the 'burbs, the barrio, and Beverly Hills, the shows set in each representing all manner of TV genres.

The beach is, of course, where the Western lifestyle has always been at its laid-back best. Its days in the TV Land sun began back with *Malibu Run*, which had a six-month run from March until September of 1961. It starred Ron Ely, who later became TV's *Tarzan*. Bailey's Landing was the fictional setting for *The Baileys of Balboa* (1964–65). Paul Ford played Captain Sam Bailey, the skipper of a battered charter boat, the *Island Princess,* which sailed concurrently with the SS *Minnow* of *Gilligan's Island*. It remained afloat for just one season. *Gidget* took us back to the beach, this time at Santa Monica, in September of 1965. Sally Field was Gidget—a character whose nickname combined the words *girl* and *midget*. She and her gang of beach buddies—Moon Doggie, Treasure, Siddo, and Larue—were surfers who rode the waves until cancellation in the spring of 1966. *Malibu U.* kept the beach theme going during the summer of 1967. Ricky Nelson starred as the dean of a college whose campus was on the beach.

*The San Pedro Beach Bums*, set on a houseboat, featured more sand, surf, and silliness. It lasted for a quick three-month run following its fall 1977 premiere. Oceanfront property was the real estate of choice for Jim Rockford of *The Rockford Files* (1973–80). The former *Maverick* played the title role of an ex-con who, after getting out of San Quentin, becomes a private eye living at 2356 Pacific Coast Highway. He eventually moved into a trailer at Paradise Cove in Malibu. Both the Paradise Cove trailer park and the Sand Castle restaurant, which figures in the series' storylines, are real places on the Malibu coastline. *Riptide* (1984–86) blended elements of *The Baileys of Balboa*, *The San Pedro Beach Bums*, and *The Rockford Files* into an hour-long show about a pair of private investigators with headquarters in a boat docked in an unspecified regional harbor. Perry King and Joe Penny (Penny became Jake of *Jake and the Fatman*, another Malibu-based character) were the partnered PI's. Anne Francis played the role of the friendly skipper of a charter boat. *Baywatch* is a romp-at-the-beach show that debuted in 1989. It focuses on Los Angeles–area lifeguard/hunks who, in turn, are tightly focused on bevies of bikinied beauties. This series, which stars David Hasselhoff (the former *Knight Rider*) and Jameson Parker (once half of *Simon and Simon*), makes *Gidget* seem as if she belonged in the Victorian era.

Theoretically, *Dragnet* coppers Friday and Gannon (Jack Webb and Harry Morgan) contended with crime wherever it occurred in the City of Angels. But it seemed as if most of their assignments kept them in the seedier districts of downtown L.A.
*Courtesy of NBC-TV.*

# BEVERLY HILLS

*The Beverly Hillbillies* helped make Beverly Hills one of the most famous places in TV Land when, after having sold their Ozark Mountain shack and its surrounding property, they moved up to 518 Crestview Drive, Beverly Hills, in 1962. They remained on their opulent estate, replete with a "cement pond," until cancellation in 1971. This series wasn't, however, the first to tie its destiny to the city surrounded by Los Angeles and fabled for its wealth and glamour. To quote from "The Ballad of Jed Clampett," Beverly Hills is the land of "swimmin' pools/movie stars." It's been the setting for TV shows for some four decades.

Its mansions, palm-lined boulevards, and affluent citizenry first came to be seen on the small screen when *The Burns and Allen Show* premiered in 1950. This comedy about the show business couple was set at their home, 312 Maple Street, Beverly Hills. Production, however, took place on sets built on a stage at the Mansfield Theater in New York City during the show's first two years. It then moved to a Hollywood studio just a few miles from the couple's actual Beverly Hills home.

Bea Benaderet and Garry Marshall were cast members. Bea later moved on to *Petticoat Junction,* where she played the owner of the Shady Rest Inn, and Garry went on to create *Happy Days*, *Laverne and Shirley*, and *Mork and Mindy*. Paul Henning, one of the show's writers, created *The Beverly Hillbillies* four years after *Burns and Allen* finished its run in 1958.

1163 Rexford Drive was the next Beverly Hills address we visited on a weekly basis. This is where *Bachelor Father* lived, from 1957 to 1962, with his thirteen-year-old niece, his Chinese houseboy, and a dog named Jasper. John Forsythe, who was to become the megabucks character Blake Carrington of *Dynasty*, had the title role in this sitcom, which had the unusual distinction of appearing on the schedules of CBS, NBC, and ABC during the course of its 157-episode run.

Two ill-fated sitcoms came along in 1987 with titles that capitalized on their settings. *Down and Out in Beverly Hills*, which was a TV version of the movie of the same name, was a sitcom featuring a wealthy family who allow a drifter to move into their mansion. It wasn't a lasting arrangement as the show, which began in the last week of July, ended in the second week of the following September. *Beverly Hills Buntz*, a spin-off of *Hill Street Blues*, starred Dennis Franz as ex-cop turned private eye Norman Buntz. It ran from November of 1987 until the third week of April 1988.

Aaron Spelling (the man responsible for the greatest number of commercial series ever produced, including *Charlie's Angels*, *The Love Boat*, *Dynasty*, *Hotel*, and many, many others) figured out how to best exploit a Beverly Hills setting. He created the first zip-coded TV series, *Beverly Hills 90210*, about a pack of teenagers (including Spelling's daughter, Tori) attending the fictitious West Beverly Hills High School. This popular, one-hour drama debuted on October 4, 1990, and launched the high-profile careers of cast members Jason Priestley, Shannen Doherty, and Luke Perry.

*The Burns and Allen Show.* George and Gracie were the best-known residents of Beverly Hills, at least they were until the Clampett clan moved in. *Courtesy of Columbia Studios.*

# NEVADA

While *Bonanza* and its Ponderosa Ranch (close by the waters of Lake Tahoe) ensure Nevada's reputation as a key part of TV Land, several other series have been set in this huge and mostly empty state.

*State Trooper*, starring Rod Cameron, was shot in Las Vegas and ran in 1957. *Blansky's Beauties* (February through June 1977) starred Nancy Walker as the manager of several Las Vegas showgirls. Scott Baio, Pat Morita (late of Milwaukee and *Happy Days*), and Rhonda Bates were in the cast. This series added Jim Belushi to its cast and was revamped and retitled as *Who's Watching the Kids?* It ran from September until the middle of December of 1978.

*Vega$*, starring Robert Urich as Las Vegas private eye Dan Tanna, utilized the city's gambling casinos and neon glitz as featured background. It had a three-year run from the fall of 1978 to the fall of 1981.

The Lake Tahoe area welcomed its second series at the end of October 1979. Shirley Jones, once the mama of *The Partridge Family*, starred in *Shirley*. It was the story of a widow who moves to Nevada with her kids to start a new life. This life didn't last long, however, as the show's last episode played on January 25, 1980. Patrick Wayne, Rosanna Arquette, and Tracy Gold (later a part of *Growing Pains*) were in the cast.

Lakes County, Nevada, was the setting for *She's the Sheriff* (1987–88). Suzanne Somers, who had left *Three's Company*, was the woman with the badge. This syndicated series was preceded by a 1983 pilot that had been rejected by CBS.

# WESTERN TV LAND BABYLON

TV Land Babylon is the one province of TV Land that shares a border with the empire of death. It is scattered about in parcels: a public sidewalk, a hotel room, the roof of a building, someone's private home. These are sites of suicide and murder . . . places where TV Land fantasy and the reality of fate blur together under the most unfortunate circumstances.

Grave Line Tours takes hearse-loads of tourists to L.A.-area cemeteries where the tombstones of once-upon-a-time stars mark plots of green grass turf as being part of TV Land. *Courtesy of Grave Line Tours.*

# The TV Land Suicide Tour Itinerary

John Belushi, that superb Killer Bee/Blues Brother/Samurai Swordsman of *Saturday Night Live* fame, died of a drug overdose at Bungalow B-3 of the Chateau Marmont Hotel on the Sunset Strip in West Hollywood, California.

Freddie Prinze, who was Chico of *Chico and the Man*, was at home when he put a fatal bullet in his head. The address is 865-75 Comstock Avenue in Westwood, where the University of California at Los Angeles is located.

*Superman* was supposed to be faster than a speeding bullet, but George Reeves, who played the man of steel, proved that such a bullet was still fatal upon impact with a mere mortal such as himself. He supposedly shot himself to death at his house at 1579 Benedict Canyon Drive in Beverly Hills, California.

Nick Adams, who played the title role of Johnny Yuma in *The Rebel,* fatally overdosed at 2126 El Roble Lane in Beverly Hills, California.

# WESTERN TV LAND GRAVE SITES

## Glendale, California
*Forest Lawn*

| | |
|---|---|
| Gracie Allen | 1906–64 |
| Lucille Ball | 1911–89 |
| Walt Disney | 1901–66 |
| Larry Fine | 1902–75 |
| Ernie Kovacs | 1914–62 |

## Burbank, California
*Valhalla Memorial Park*

| | |
|---|---|
| Bea Benaderet | 1894–1968 |
| Oliver Hardy | 1892–1957 |

*Hillside Memorial Park*

| | |
|---|---|
| Jack Benny | 1894–1974 |

## Los Angeles, California
*Westwood Village Memorial Park*

| | |
|---|---|
| Jim Backus | 1913–89 |
| Sebastian Cabot | 1918–77 |

*Calvary Cemetery*

| | |
|---|---|
| Lou Costello | 1906–59 |

*Forest Lawn—L.A. Hills*

| | |
|---|---|
| Liberace | 1911–87 |

*Eden Memorial Park*

| | |
|---|---|
| Groucho Marx | 1890–77 |

## Los Angeles County, California
*Inglewood—Inglewood Park Cemetery*

| | |
|---|---|
| Edgar Bergen | 1903–78 |

*Culver City—Holy Cross Cemetery*

| | |
|---|---|
| Jackie Coogan | 1914–84 |

## Montana
*Captin—Smokey the Bear Historical State Park*

Smokey the Bear

Capes were merely fashion statements
and never of any practical use for
Batman, Robin, and Cat Woman.
They presumably made getting in
and out of the Batmobile, or riding
the Batcycle, a more unpleasant experience than need be.    *Courtesy of 20th
Century-Fox TV.*

# WESTERN TV LAND GEOGRAPHIA

## The Bat Cave

The Bat Cave is where Batman/Bruce Wayne (played by Adam West) and the Boy Wonder, Robin/Dick Grayson (played by Burt Ward), hid their Batmobile. It is, perhaps, the most renowned of all underground TV Land locations. While there is general agreement that the Bat Cave was fourteen miles from downtown Gotham City, its actual location remains a controversy argued over by TV Land historians and journalists. Historians say the cave was built in a Desilu Studios soundstage that was destroyed by fire after *Batman* (1966–68) was canceled. Newspaper reports, however, contend that the Bat Cave is actually Bronson Cave, a natural formation found in Los Angeles's Griffith Park.

## Herded on the Grapevine

Jane Wyman, Robert Foxworth, Abby Dalton, and Lorenzo Lamas all played leading characters on *Falcon Crest*—a prime-time serial (1981–90) set in Northern California's wine country. The show's exteriors were shot at Spring Mountain Vineyards in St. Helena. This real-life wine producer marketed two *Falcon Crest*–labeled wines in 1982.

## Dream Vacation

*Fantasy Island* (1978–84) starred Ricardo Montalban as the mysterious proprietor Mr. Roarke and Herve Villechaize as his assistant, Tattoo. The show was filmed in a tropical paradise but not on an island. Its location was a botanical park called The Arboretum, which is twenty-five miles from downtown Los Angeles.

## On the Mother Road

*Route 66* ended its network run in 1964. By 1984, most of the historic U.S. Highway 66 had either been bypassed or replaced by a new Interstate. One section that still remains intact runs through Kingman, Arizona, and is called Andy Devine Drive to honor the Kingman native who became famous as a TV Land cowboy sidekick and, later, as a kiddie-show host. The Route 66 Distillery, a Kingman eatery, still serves a Tod and Buzz Burger.

## Dueling Detectives: PI's in the Sky

The Century Plaza Towers are twin skyscrapers located at 2029 and 2049 Century Park East, in the Century City area of Los Angeles. Two of TV Land's premier private investigative agencies are located here: the Blue Moon Detective Agency of *Moonlighting* and the offices of *Remington Steele*.

## Lasting Impressions

Mann's Chinese Theater (at 6925 Hollywood Boulevard in Hollywood) is famous for its collection of cast-in-wet-cement hand- and footprints made by many film and TV stars. The most unique impressions are, however, of neither hand nor foot. They were made by Jimmy Durante's nose and the webbed feet of Donald Duck.

## Treasures

Nevada has two museums that preserve various icons and artifacts of TV Land. It sounds like quite an all-star party at Bethany's Celebrity Doll and Wax Museum in Las Vegas. You can say hello to those who are jolly dollies and those who have been waxed poetic: the casts of *Saturday Night Live* and *Gilligan's Island*, some of *Charlie's Angels*, Cher, Sam Kinison, one of the regulars from *Full House* . . . over 3,000 celebrities are all gathered under one roof. Also in Las Vegas is the Liberace Museum. The Piano Man of TV Land left enough kitsch to be remembered by to fill a few cargo containers. His museum exhibits his flamboyant costumes, cars, gold and platinum records, and a gold casting of his hands.

The Philo Farnsworth Museum, in Philo's hometown of Rigby, Idaho, honors the man considered to be the "Father of Television." Farnsworth is said to have gotten the notion about TV scan lines while plowing parallel rows of potatoes. His memory and inventiveness are honored by the tiny museum, which holds a collection of television tubes, awards, and some of Farnsworth's personal items.

The Lucille Ball Pavilion is the place to pay homage to the Queen of TV Land comedy. A trove of Lucy memorabilia is on display at this museum located at Universal Studios in Los Angeles.

# REALLY GOING TO—

## Twin Peaks

Located somewhere between the border of *The Twilight Zone* and the frontier of *The Outer Limits* is a place called *Twin Peaks*. It's also about thirty miles east of Seattle. This outlandish, prime-time soap was created by movie director David Lynch and his partner, Mark Frost. Kyle MacLachlan starred as FBI agent Dale Cooper. Michael Ontkean (once one of *The Rookies*) played Sheriff Harry S. Truman. Richard Beymer, Sherilyn Fenn, Lara Flynn Boyle, Joan Chen, Russ Tamblyn, and Piper Laurie were also members of the show's huge cast. *Twin Peaks* ran from April of 1990 through the spring of 1991. Despite the show's cancellation, tourists still regularly arrive here, by the chartered busload, from as far away as Europe and Asia. Peakers, as fanat-

ics of the show are proud to be called, make these pilgrimages only to find that parts of the brooding, mythical TV town are spread across a collection of real-life mountain hamlets and lumber towns in this Northwest corner of TV Land. As FBI agent Dale Cooper discovered, it is a place well worth checking out.

## Principal Physical Features

*Mount Si*
It's the region's connections to the mystical world that many Peakers are most curious to explore. While the local police chief does not, like Agent Cooper, throw rocks at a bottle as part of his criminal investigations, and while no one has yet verified any actual visitations made by a fire-dancing, one-armed Bob, a historical link that connects this area with the supernatural does exist. Native Americans have long regarded Mount Si, which looms high above the region, as a holy site.

*Snoqualmie Falls*
Located just outside the city limits of Snoqualmie, the falls' misty visage is prominently featured in the show's opening credits. One hundred feet higher than Niagara Falls, its flow plunges in a drop that stretches for 286 feet.

## Principal Attractions

*The Great Northern Hotel*
When Agent Cooper asked Sheriff Harry S. Truman to recommend a simple, inexpensive hotel ("All I need is a bed, a bathroom, a telephone, and sometimes a television"), the sheriff responded, "I can get you a good rate up at the Great Northern." The exteriors of the Salish Lodge, which has ninety-one rooms and overlooks Snoqualmie Falls, was used to depict the fictional hotel.

Unlike its TV counterpart, the Salish is neither simple nor inexpensive. Located on the outskirts of Snoqualmie Falls, each of its rooms is equipped with a fireplace and a Jacuzzi.

### The Mar T Cafe

*Twin Peaks* became incorporated as part of TV Land in 1989, when director David Lynch made his first visit here. Soon after having swallowed his first sip of "damn good coffee" at the Mar T Cafe, *Twin Peaks* began evolving into the darkest and most mysterious of all the many provinces of TV Land. The Mar T, which was called the RR Diner in the show, is in the town of North Bend. It's also the place where the director experienced an epiphany upon tasting a slice of its home-baked cherry pie. The Mar T now sells more cherry pies than any other establishment in the state of Washington.

> *"Diane, that cherry pie is worth going out of your way for."*
>
> •
>
> *"This must be where pies go when they die."*
>
> —FBI Agent Dal Cooper

### The Laura Palmer Murder Scene

The late, lovely Laura was done in at the Niblock Rail Yard which, though close by the Salish Lodge, is on land belonging to the Puget Sound and Snoqualmie Valley Railroad. The crime was committed in a battered green rail car.

### The Laura Palmer Corpse Discovery Location

The plastic-wrapped body washed ashore near the Kiana Lodge in Poulsbo. The Kiana's interiors doubled for those of the Great Northern Hotel as well as for the Blue Lake Lodge, where the Martells and Josie Packard lived.

*The Ronette Pulaski Crime Scene*
Ronette wasn't killed; she was brutally attacked but managed to survive, though only to be forgotten in episodes subsequent to her assault. The scene of this crime may be viewed at the train trestle found at the intersection of 396 Drive and Reinig Road, in Snoqualmie Falls.

*The Roadhouse Bar*
The exterior of the Colonial Inn, located in Fall City (just northwest of Snoqualmie Falls), doubled for the show's Roadhouse Bar.
Also in Fall City, on the Preston–Fall City Road, is a kite shop called Streamers. It doesn't have the gas pumps or signs seen in the show but it doubled as the site of the Gas Farm.

## Other Sights Worth a Peaker's Quick Peek

Mount Si High doubled for Twin Peaks High, the school in which Laura Palmer was elected homecoming queen. The big log and the town square's gazebo, both seen in the show's opening credits, are on Railroad Avenue in Snoqualmie Falls.

# Shopping in Twin Peaks

Shopping for *Twin Peaks* souvenirs is a paramount activity for every Peaker.

In Snoqualmie Falls, there's a Victorian gift shop called Isadora's, which sells *Twin Peaks* maps. Hungry sightseers will find a reasonably digestible sort of memento, the *Twin Peaks* burger, on the menu at the nearby Big Edd's Family Restaurant.

In North Bend, just a block away from the Mar T Cafe, the Alpine Blossom Floral Shop gladly accepts money from those mesmerized by the Laura Palmer murder mystery. The shop stocks commemorative T-shirts, tapes, postcards, buttons, caps, and nowhere-else-to-be-found Log Lady logs at $4.95 each.

# Bedrock

*The Flintstones*, the first cartoon series to appear on a prime-time network schedule, was an animated takeoff on *The Honeymooners*. It appealed to adults as well as kids. The half-hour show was set in Bedrock, a suburban community of the Stone Age—which means that Bedrock must be the most ancient of places in TV Land.

According to TV cartoon lore, Bedrock (population 2,500) dates back 1,000,040 years. The series premiered in 1960 and ran until September of 1966; subsequent versions of it (one-hour specials, Saturday morning shows, spin-offs, etc.) have appeared ever since, and the original strip continues to play in

syndication. In 1972, entrepreneur Hudi Speckels built a tourist attraction known as Bedrock City/Grand Canyon, Arizona.

## Bedrock Today

An immense likeness of Fred Flintstone, with his left arm uplifted and hand pointing to a sign reading "Yabba-Dabba-Doo Welcome," marks the entrance to Bedrock City near Williams, Arizona. This mock municipality spreads out over forty acres of the state's northern, hardscrabble land. The neo-prehistoric commu-

Fred Flintstone looms a great deal larger than life at the entrance to Bedrock City. *Courtesy of Linda Speckels.*

The house that Fred Flintstone called home looks a lot like the cosmic egg in which Mork descended from Ork to Earth.
*Courtesy of Linda Speckels.*

nity includes a walk-through theme park that showcases the Flintstone and Rubble domiciles. They're completely furnished with period pieces reflecting the taste and style of Bedrock's Golden Age.

Other pseudo-relic structures in town are the Stonehead General Store, the Dinogas Station, and the Bedrock Movie Theater, which runs Flintstone cartoons. Statues of the community's stalwarts, some of which talk and all of whom stand still for picture-taking, are strategically scattered within the city limits. Apart from the occasional Flintstones' fan on pilgrimage to this prehistoric TV Land landmark, it's the Grand Canyon camping crowd that comes to visit.

When the RV parks fill up, Bedrock City offers the closest-to-the-Canyon alternative for spending the night. Facilities include campgrounds, a gift shop, and Fred's Diner. And, as if all this wasn't enough to make Bedrock an irresistible destination, it's the only place where travelers can get food, drink, and access to a flushing toilet between the area's main highway and the Grand Canyon's south rim. Adults might wish that their RVs were parked in some Las Vegas casino lot, but the Pebbles and Bamm-Bamm peer group will find Bedrock to be a super stopover.

## Getting There

The address of Bedrock City is Junction 180 & 64, Grand Canyon Highway, Star Route, Williams, Arizona 86046. The telephone number is (602)635-2600.

# Rocky and Bullwinkle Emporium

A flying rodent known as Rocket J. Squirrel and his pal, a moose named Bullwinkle, entered the pantheon of TV cartoon heroes in November of 1959. Their show, originally titled *Rocky and His Friends*, was created by Jay Ward—an offbeat genius of animation who had previously gifted TV Land with the presence of *Crusader Rabbit*.

Rocky and Bullwinkle were good guys who were forever battling the evil forces of a pair of no-goodniks named Boris Badenov and Natasha Fatale. According to the show, Rocky hailed from the fictitious town of Frostbite Falls, Minnesota, and Moosylvania was Bullwinkle's native land. While both of these locales are obviously impossible to find, a shrine that celebrates these two characters (and other Jay Ward creations—a gang that includes George of the Jungle, Super Chicken, Dudley Do-Right, Snidely Whiplash, Inspector Fenwick and daughter Nell, as well as Mr. Peabody, the world's smartest dog, and his pet boy Sherman) can all be found in The Dudley Do-Right Emporium.

The place would be easy to miss if not for its landmark...a fifteen-foot-tall statue of Bullwinkle, in whose outstretched hand sits the renowned Rocky. Opened in 1971, operated by Billie Ward (Jay's widow), the store is nearly as eccentric as the characters themselves. Merchandise celebrating the Rocky and Bullwinkle phenomenon includes T-shirts, sweatshirts, gym shorts, greeting cards, buttons, posters and stickers adorned with the cartoon characters' likenesses, and other collectibles. This shop, somewhat set back from the world-famous Sunset Strip at 8218 Sunset Boulevard, West Hollywood, California 90046, is open on Tuesdays, Wednesdays, and Thursdays. Mail orders are accepted.

# Lawrence Welk Village

Lawrence Welk, the King of Champagne Music and the Maestro of TV Land, retired from television in 1982 and died ten years later. There's hardly a chance, however, that he won't be very long remembered. He began insuring the permanency of his legacy in 1965, when he opened a motel and restaurant bearing his name in California's northern San Diego County. This complex is quite different from the modest still-standing sod house where Welk grew up in Starsburg, North Dakota.

Over the course of ensuing decades, Welk demonstrated that he was as adept an entrepreneur as he was a TV bandleader. He expanded his original holdings into a multifaceted operation that now includes (in addition to the Lawrence Welk Restaurant): a mobile home park called Champagne Village; the time-sharing Lawrence Welk Resort with its Lawrence Welk Hotel; the Lawrence Welk Dinner Theater; the Lawrence Welk Gift Gallery; the Lawrence Welk Music and Video Center; the Lawrence Welk Museum (featuring the world's largest champagne glass); the Lawrence Welk Shopping Plaza; plus golf courses. The bronze, life-size Lawrence Welk Statue stands in the resort complex's main plaza, close by the intersection of Champagne Boulevard and Lawrence Welk Drive.

The exact address of all this wealth of Welkdom is 8860 Lawrence Welk Drive, Escondido, California. The museum is open daily (10 A.M. to 1 P.M. and 4:30 P.M. to 7:30 P.M.), and admission is free.

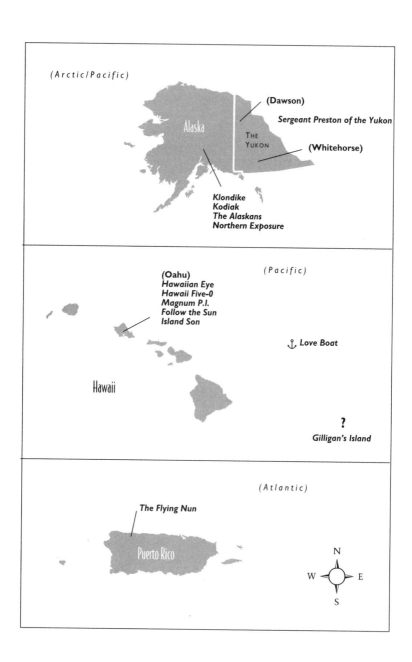

(Arctic/Pacific)

Alaska

THE YUKON

(Dawson)
Sergeant Preston of the Yukon

(Whitehorse)

Klondike
Kodiak
The Alaskans
Northern Exposure

(Oahu)
Hawaiian Eye
Hawaii Five-0
Magnum P.I.
Follow the Sun
Island Son

(Pacific)

⚓ Love Boat

Hawaii

?
Gilligan's Island

(Atlantic)

The Flying Nun

Puerto Rico

N
W ✦ E
S

# FAR-FLUNG TV LAND

TV Land is neither confined to the contiguous United States, nor to its national boundaries, nor by international borders. It has become an entity of global dimensions with outposts in Alaska, Hawaii, Puerto Rico, Canada, Mexico, Australia, Europe, Asia, and Africa. . . .

Due to American military involvement in world affairs, soldiers and sailors have raised the TV Land flag wherever they've been posted. *The Rat Patrol* (1966–68), though it was filmed in Spain, was an American armored car force that fought Germany's Afrika Korps on the sand-swept battlefields of the Sahara Desert.

*Hogan's Heroes* (1965–71) were the confined residents of Germany's World War II POW camp known as Stalag 13. It boasted a steam room and services provided by a barber as well as a French chef.

*McHale's Navy* was based, from the fall of 1962 until the fall of 1965, on the fictional South Pacific isle of Taratupa. Then this squadron of misfits (which included Ernest Borgnine, Tim Conway and, for a couple of years, future *Love Boat* captain Gavin

MacLeod) was transferred to World War II's European theater and stationed outside of the contrived Voltafiore, Italy, until the series ended in August of 1966.

Wars in Asia brought TV Land servicemen and women across the Pacific to deal with the conflicts engendered by Communist expansion. *M★A★S★H* was set near the conceived city of Ouijongbu, South Korea . . . close to the front-line hostilities of the Korean War.

A signpost in the *M★A★S★H* compound indicated that it was some 6,133 miles away from Toledo, Ohio. The show's exterior scenes were shot at the 20th Century-Fox Ranch (now California's Malibu State Park), while interiors were filmed at Fox Studios, where the compound occupied a 45-by-90-foot set that included a Korean landscape scene as its backdrop.

Alan Alda, Mike Farrell, Loretta ("Hot Lips" Houlihan) Swit, and McLean Stevenson starred...as did Harry Morgan (once the Pete of *Pete and Gladys* as well as Joe Friday's former *Dragnet* sidekick, Bill Gannon) and Jamie Farr as Maxwell Klinger— a corporal who took up cross-dressing in hopes that it would cause the

*McHale's Navy.* Sure they were stationed out in the South Pacific somewhere, but for all the Pentagon knew, the silliest sailors in World War II might as well have been based on Gilligan's Island. *Courtesy of ABC-TV.*

The sign of the times indicates that the M★A★S★H cast was soldiering on during the years when the Korean War was waged. *Courtesy of Paramount Studios.*

army to discharge him. Farr was the sole cast member who served in the real Korean War. M★A★S★H ran for eleven years (1972–83), while the Korean War itself ran for three.

The next Asian land war inspired two network series. Both *Tour of Duty* (1987–89) and *China Beach* (1988–90) were set in Vietnam. *Tour of Duty* was set near Saigon and filmed in Hawaii for its first season, and then in California for its last. *China Beach* was set at an American military hospital and recreational complex in Da Nang, South Vietnam. Like M★A★S★H, this series was shot at Malibu Canyon State Park.

# ALASKA

The Gold Rush of 1897–99 was initially responsible for prompting TV Land to expand into Alaska. A character named Silky Harris, played by Roger Moore, was our guide to the region. His series, *The Alaskans*, was set in Skagway and was shot on location. It ran from 1959 to 1960, when poor ratings lead to the show being entirely revamped and relocated very far to the south—all the way to Mexico—where it re-emerged as *Acapulco*.

James Coburn, as adventurer and hotel owner Jeff Durain, took up where Moore had left off. His series, *Klondike*, was also set in Skagway and was about the Gold Rush era. It ran from 1960 to 1961.

The third man to lead us into TV Land's most northerly turf was Clint Walker (formerly the cowboy called *Cheyenne*). Walker starred in *Kodiak*, portraying the role of an officer of the Alaska State Patrol. His job was to cover 50,000 square miles of ice and snow by means of four-wheel-drive truck, snowmobile, skis, and snowshoes. He only lasted one month on the job, as this shot-on-location series began in September 1974 and ended in October of the same year.

*Facing page:* He's Not Even Wearing Thermal Underwear! Warm weather fashion for the Royal Mounted Police, as modeled here by Sergeant Preston of the Yukon, makes Preston look personable. No matter how warm the weather, however, the man never truly warmed up to anyone but his dog, King. His first name, Frank, was never uttered in any of the series' episodes. *Courtesy of Wrather Corp.*

# THE YUKON

In 1955, TV Land spread north over an international border, past fifty degrees latitude, and into Canada's Yukon Territory. *Sergeant Preston of the Yukon* (who remained on patrol until 1958) introduced us to the settlements of Dawson and Whitehorse and the surrounding frozen terrain. What we were really seeing, though, was Colorado, as the show was shot near the town of Ashcroft.

He probably could never have gotten there (or anywhere else in the frozen north) without the help of his dogsled team and most especially his lead dog, Yukon King. When it wasn't dogsled weather, Preston rode his horse Rex.

## Owning a Patch of Snow

You can't just buy property in *The Big Valley* or move into *Mister Rogers's Neighborhood*, but in 1955, when Sergeant Preston and King made their successful move from radio to television, anyone could acquire a bit of real TV land real estate. The series celebrated the romance of the

Royal Canadian Mounted Police and the Klondike Gold Rush and put the Yukon Territory on the TV Land map.

Celebrating the show's popularity, and hoping to cash in on it, the show's sponsor, the Quaker Oats Company, endeavored to put bits of the Yukon into the real estate portfolios of millions of fans.

After negotiating with the Canadian government, Quaker Oats bought 19.11 acres of land on the Yukon River for $10,000. They subdivided their new holdings, a dozen miles from Dawson, into 21 million plots that measured one square-inch apiece. They printed up 21 million deeds and included coupons redeemable for the deeds in boxes of their cereal. Oatmeal-eating fans of the show were urged to mail in these coupons and become bonafide, micro-mini TV Land barons. Thousands responded to this Arctic land-grab promotion.

One particularly enthusiastic fan, of both Sergeant Preston and Quaker Oats, claimed to have collected ten thousand of these deeds, which he believed entitled him to a seventy-five-square-foot piece of property. His land claim was subsequently denied, however, because his holdings were judged to be non-contiguous.

The Quaker promotion was so popular that the company followed it up with a second TV Land giveaway. This time, purchasers of one-ounce packages of Puffed Oats or Puffed Rice were offered the opportunity to receive one-ounce containers of Yukon dirt. Unfortunately, owning TV Land real estate proved to be only a temporary reality. The Canadian government was forced to foreclose on the properties when Quaker Oats failed to pay their bill of $37.00 they owed for back taxes! Those 1955 deeds are currently worth approximately $50.00 each to collectors.

# HAWAII

The fiftieth state has lent its name to three series and has been the locale of several more since becoming a part of TV Land. *Hawaiian Eye* (1959–63) was a detective series set in Honolulu, which formed a triumvirate with its sister shows *Surfside Six* (in Miami Beach) and *77 Sunset Strip* (in Los Angeles). Robert Conrad and Anthony Eisley were the private eyes, and Connie Stevens portrayed a nightclub singer named Cricket who performed at the Hawaiian Village Hotel's Shell Bar.

*Hawaii Five-0* (1968–80) starred Jack Lord and James MacArthur in TV's most lasting crime series. It was shot entirely on location. *Hawaiian Heat*, about two Chicago cops who went to work for the Honolulu Police Department, didn't fare as well. It ran from September 1984 until the close of that year.

*Follow the Sun*, another Honolulu-based series, was about the exploits of two free-lance writers. They were played by Barry Coe and Brett Halsey. This series ran during the 1961–62 TV season.

*Island Son* (1989–90) was set at Kamehameha Medical Center in Honolulu. Richard Chamberlain, who had been *Dr. Kildare*, played Dr. Daniel Kulani in this series.

*Magnum P.I.* (1980–88), which starred Tom Selleck in the title role, was shot at the same facilities that had formerly been the production center for *Hawaii Five-0*. A pair of Dobermans named Zeus and Apollo and the voice of Orson Welles complemented the show's casting.

# Gilligan's Island

Aside from crime shows, and the reincarnation of *Dr. Kildare* as an islander, Hawaii's principal connection with TV Land was made via *Gilligan's Island* (1964–67). The first pilot of this absurd sitcom was shot on the Hawaiian island of Kauai. The motion picture *South Pacific* had been filmed in the same area some years before Gilligan and his mates were shipwrecked here. The pilot was judged to be unacceptable and a second one was produced on Zuma Beach, near Malibu.

A third and final *Gilligan's Island* was conceived after the series was given a green light for broadcast. An artificial island in the middle of an artificial lake was created, at a cost of $75,000, at the CBS Studio Center in Los Angeles's San Fernando Valley. While the Captain and Mr. and Mrs. Howell have passed on to TV Land heaven, the rest of the *Minnow's* passengers theoretically remain on the island awaiting yet another call for a TV Reunion Special.

## Known Geographical Facts About the Castaways
• Mrs. Howell was from Grosse Pointe, Michigan.
• Ginger came from Hollywood, California.
• The Professor hailed from Cleveland, Ohio.
• Mary Ann's roots are in Plainville, Kansas.

## Note: The People Demand . . .
In 1992, the governor of Hawaii was presented with a petition of 30,000 names which requested that the island of Maui be officially renamed Gilligan's Island.

# TV LAND IN OUTER SPACE

## Krypton

The initial "strange visitor" was, of course, *Superman*. He hailed from the exploded planet of Krypton and entered TV Land in 1953. After spending his boyhood with adopted human parents on a farm outside of Smallville, he became a reporter on a great metropolitan newspaper—*The Daily Planet* of Metropolis. *Superman* took a flier from first-run syndication in 1957.

## Mars

Uncle Martin, who was *My Favorite Martian*, crash-landed after a flight took him to TV Land from his home planet of Mars in 1963. He settled in Los Angeles and managed to escape from a weekly broadcast grind in 1966.

If a Martian were to come to Earth, where would he go to best fit in? Uncle Martin (played by Ray Walston) showed he was one smart Martian by landing in Los Angeles.
*Courtesy of CBS-TV.*

# Ork

Mork left his native planet of Ork and came down to live in TV Land to investigate our culture in 1978. Boulder, Colorado, was his home-away-from-home until *Mork and Mindy* ceased production in the summer of 1982.

Mork moved into Mindy's manse in Boulder, Colorado, soon after arriving from outer space.
*Courtesy of ABC-TV.*

*Lost in Space.* June Lockhart, perhaps feeling fed-up after playing the third-banana role to a boy and his dog (Lassie), married the former Zorro and became the mother of the Robinson family. Headed for Alpha Centauri, she and her family blasted-off into Outer Space (along with the evil stowaway, Dr. Smith) in the early 1960s. The Robinsons got lost, of course, and nobody could ever find them. If they had only brought Lassie along, well, chances are she would have lead them back home to Earth.
*Courtesy of 20th Century-Fox.*

# Melmac

*ALF* (which stands for Alien Life Form) hit the solid ground of TV Land in the Fall of 1986. While *ALF* was a furry species and had no physical similarities in common with preceding aliens, there were a couple of parallels between his visitation and those made before him. Like the Martian's, Alf's space transport went out of control and crash-landed. And just as *Superman* could never return to Krypton because it detonated into smithereens drifting in the solar breeze, so, too, did *ALF*'s home planet of Melmac explode soon after his launching. *ALF* disappeared from TV screens in 1991.

The Jetsons lived in TV Land's highly civilized blue yonder of the future.
*Courtesy of Universal TV.*

# FAR-FLUNG TV LAND *GEOGRAPHIA*

## A Ways into Africa

Africa became part of TV Land in 1955, when *Jungle Jim* went on the air. Johnny Weissmuller played the title role of a guide who was assisted by a chimp named Tamba. *Jungle Boy* joined Jim on the airwaves in 1958. Boy was a fourteen-year-old who, as the sole survivor of an airplane crash, grew up as a wild child. This show was filmed in Kenya. *Daktari* (1966–69) was set at the fictitious Wameru Game Preserve and Research Center. Marshall Thompson starred as veterinarian Dr. Marsh Tracy. The series was shot at California's Africa, U.S.A.—a preserve for wild animals built by Ivan Tors and Ralph Helfer. *Tarzan* came to television in 1966 and stayed until 1968. Ron Ely was *Tarzan* (a.k.a. Lord Greystoke). The show was shot in Mexico and Brazil.

## Into India

TV Land penetrated into the tropical interior of India during the 1952–53 season as *Ramar of the Jungle* rode into view atop an elephant.

*Opposite:* Sally Field, as Sister Bertrille, got a lift from the tropical breezes that favor the island of Puerto Rico, where her convent was located. Note: Mother Superior never confused her airborne charge with an angel no matter how high the sister might soar.  *Courtesy of ABC-TV.*

## Holy Island Has Commonwealth Status

While Puerto Rico has maintained its status as a commonwealth and has not become one of the United States, it did join TV Land in 1967. That's when Sally Field became Elsie Ethrington, who was ordained as Sister Bertrille—*The Flying Nun*. She flew, and served God, at the Convent San Tanco in San Juan. The sister flew off to God-knows-where in 1970, after receiving her network cancellation.

As Star Fleet's First Officer Spock of the *Enterprise,* Leonard Nimoy was on a mission to explore brave new worlds. In *Mission: Impossible,* he had to make covert and highly implausible, if not impossible, things happen. Not many characters born in TV Land can boast of having served both the planet and the entire Universe during the course of their career. *Courtesy of CBS-TV.*

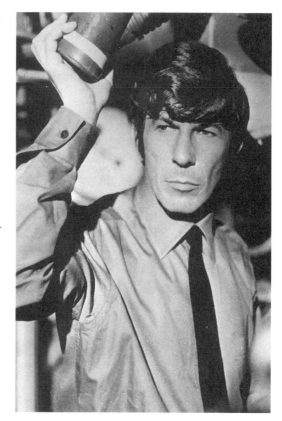

## Impossible Nations

The most far-flung of all territories of Far-Flung TV Land are those that exist in the make-believe of *Mission: Impossible.* These never-to-be-nations include Svardia, Republic of Camagua, Santales, and the Eastern European Republic of Lagosia.

# REALLY GOING TO—

# Northern Exposure

In the paradoxical geography of TV Land, the remote Alaskan village of Cicely can be reached by a mere two-hour drive from Seattle. According to standard maps, however, this destination is really the town of Roslyn, Washington. Roslyn is the real-life Cicely—the setting for *Northern Exposure*, a series that debuted in July of 1990. This series, about a New York City doctor who's relocated to the wilds of the fiftieth state, stars Rob Morrow, Janine Turner, Barry Corbin, Cynthia Geary, and John Corbett.

Chosen by the show's producers for its folksy atmosphere, Roslyn underwent a few cosmetic changes to make it look more like an Alaskan settlement than the Pacific Northwest community it is. Totem poles were erected on a number of street corners and antlers were affixed to some storefronts.

An estimated five to fifteen thousand fans come each year to Cicely/Roslyn to visit the Roslyn Cafe, the location used for the office of Dr. Joel Fleischman and that of radio station KBHR. The other local landmarks worth seeing are The Oasis and The Brick.

## Roslyn/Cicely Connections

- As per TV Land history, Cicely was named by a woman named Roslyn—one of the show's principal characters—who named it as a tribute to her lesbian lover.

- Roslyn has a population of 986, while there are 840 residing in Cicely. That means 146 people disappear when Roslyn becomes Cicely. Nobody knows where these folks go off to, though *Twin Peaks* is the most likely place. The land of the Log Lady is but an hour's distance to the west.

## Take a Bus

Gray Line of Seattle operates a daily bus tour, from May through October, which takes passengers on a seven-hour journey to *Northern Exposure* territory and then on to the twin towns that are the settings for *Twin Peaks*. The cost is $30.00 for adults; $15.00 for kids two to twelve years old. Call 1-800-426-7532 for reservations.

# The Village

A place known only as "the Village" was the setting for *The Prisoner*, a bleak and brutish and oh-so-very British TV series. It had a seventeen-episode run on American television in 1968. The Village is a nameless community in which prisoners are called by numbers only. The series was conceived by its star, the former *Secret Agent* man, Patrick McGoohan.

*The Prisoner* was laden with symbolism and cynicism alike. The Village was where kidnap victims were brought, from all over the world, to spend the remainders of their lives. All of them had been intelligence agents, operatives who authorities had come to consider threatening, each deemed as being someone who "knew too much."

A place of no escape, the Village is TV Land's Elba, updated with electronic eavesdropping and brainwashing techniques advanced by the twentieth century. The Village is bordered by thick forest, forbidding mountains, and shimmering sea. Its polyglot architecture reflects far-flung cultures by using towers and turrets, spires and domes. Houses painted in Crayola colors dot the coastline. This self-contained world includes a variety of civic amenities: parks and theaters, a hospital and cemetery, a castle, and a Palace of Fun. There is a postal service, but the mail only goes across town. All phone calls are local. Taxis ply the streets but go no further than the municipal limits.

This is the dark side of TV Land . . . a place where the likes of Napoleon Solo (*The Man From U.N.C.L.E.*) and, most certainly, both Maxwell Smart and Agent 99 (*Get Smart*) would be sure to crack. Kafkaesque and Orwellian, the Village also reverberated with Ayn Rand–like symbolism and imagery that might have (but didn't) originated with Fellini. McGoohan shot his show in a location that he (like such accomplished men as Bertrand Russell, Noel Coward and George Bernard Shaw) had come to know as a resort and artistic refuge. This resort is the Hotel Portmeiron, an eccentric masterpiece built by an amateur architect called Clough Williams-Ellis.

Its grounds are the site of annual conventions staged by fans of *The Prisoner*. Those who seek to visit the Hotel Portmeiron will find it on Cardigan Bay, in the north of Wales, near the town of Penrhyndeudraeth.

# The *Twin Peaks* of Japan

Japan's fascination with its cross-cultural connection to *Twin Peaks* has lead to the unprecedented establishment of a TV Land enclave in the heart of the Land of the Rising Sun. This enclave is called

Matsue—a small town set in a region of verdant, rolling hills, which is promoted as the Japanese *Twin Peaks.*

Theater manager Tai Hajime, the man responsible for the promotion, bases the linkage on this observation:

> *"We've got a mysterious atmosphere, a sense of utter nothingness, and even waterfalls, just like in the TV series."*

Matsue is six hours by train from Tokyo. Stations all along the route between the city and the town are plastered with posters that feature Matsue's lush image and an inset photo of FBI Agent Dale Cooper talking into his Dictaphone and recording this comment: "Your Twin Peaks might be there."

Ever since becoming aware of *Twin Peaks,* the Japanese people have amply demonstrated their fascination with its mystique in a variety of ways . . .

- Over thirty thousand sets of *Twin Peaks* videos were sold (at $440 per fourteen-episode set) almost immediately after going on sale.
- *How To Be a Peaker* and *White Paper on Twin Peaks Psychoanalysis* have been big sellers in bookstores across the country.
- "How To Enjoy Watching Twin Peaks" is a very popular seminar that offers participants the opportunity to explore such intricacies as the hidden dynamics involved in the relationship between Nadine and the Log Lady.
- Despite a $2,000 price tag, Japan Travel Bureau's five-day package tour of the *Twin Peaks* region is a hot-ticket item. It features a visit to The Rock—the place where Laura Palmer's body washed up on the riverbank. Plastic body bags are issued here, so tourists can get inside them and snap photos of each other while mimicking the dead girl's pose.
- Thousands of people come to Tokyo's Shinjuku Station to lay

wreaths at the Rora Pama Altar—a shrine decorated with photos of Laura Palmer.

- *Twin Peaks* terminology has become part of the Japanese lexicon. *Pika* is the word used to denote a typical fan of the show; extremely demonstrative fans are called *TP furiku*, which translates as *Twin Peaks freaks*.

# TOTAL
# TV
# LAND

*Harry O.* David Janssen, who was "Richard Diamond: Private Eye" before he was Dr. Richard Kimble (a.k.a. "The Fugitive"), went back to work as a TV Land detective known as Harry Orwell. "Harry O" was a San Diego cop who took a bullet in the back and decided to quit the force; Harry also quit San Diego when the setting of the show was switched to L.A. in the middle of its first season.
*Courtesy of WB-TV.*

# TV LAND TRAVEL

Folks have been on the move throughout TV Land ever since its inception. They've traveled by foot, been pulled by horses, been propelled over water by wind and paddles, been driven on rails and over roads by the power of engines generating steam or fueled by gasoline, diesel, and even nuclear fuel.

## Searchers, Nomads, and Those on the Run

TV Land's most noteworthy shows about such itinerant types include . . .

### The Rebel (October 1959–September 1961)

Nick Adams played Johnny Yuma who, as the song says, "was a rebel/ and he roamed through the West." It may have been a particularly vague itinerary, but Yuma, a defeated Confederate soldier, didn't really have anything better to do at the end of the Civil War. The South was in ruins. He probably figured that Yankee carpetbaggers were on the way to rip him off. There wasn't any local Scarlett O'Hara–type for him to stick around for, so he split. He didn't bother getting rid of his Confederate uniform or replacing his heavy boots with walking shoes. Johnny Yuma traveled very light, carrying neither a suitcase nor as much as an overnight bag. He didn't take a map along, either.

# A Man Called Shenandoah (September 1965-September 1966)

Robert Horton was Shenandoah—an assumed name taken by a man who had been shot by unknown assailants in the mid-1800s. He would have bled to death if it wasn't for a couple of bounty hunters who just happened to be on their way across the prairie when they spotted him and recognized that he'd soon be a vulture treat if they didn't intervene. The bounty hunters brought him to a saloon, where he regained consciousness. It didn't take long for him to realize he had amnesia and, consequently, no idea who he was, or where he'd been, or where he might have been going. He spent thirty-four prime-time half-hours stumbling around the frontier looking for answers.

# Route 66 (October 1960-September 1964)

Tod Stiles and Buzz Murdock (played by Martin Milner and George Maharis) were pals who both had one-track minds centered on vehicular movement. Some TV scholars have suggested that these two young men may have overdosed on Jack Kerouac and were likewise inspired to "See the U.S.A./ in a Chevrolet" by Chevy's catchy TV commercials of the time. The simple TV-truth is, however, that Tod and Buzz never stopped driving their Corvette Stingray from East to West: one little town to the next. They stopped only for gas, a night's sleep, and, perhaps, a little work for pocket change, or maybe just long enough to solve some pressing local problem. Fortunately, they weren't likely to get lost, as they always stuck to Route 66. Route 66 used to run between Chicago and Los Angeles, but they had no destination for the road to take them to. They spent all their time in on-the-road, prime-time inertia.

# Kung Fu (October 1972–June 1975)

Kwai Chang Caine (David Carradine) was born in China and raised in a Shaolin temple. After assassinating a member of the royal family he escaped to America, where he attempted to track his long-lost half-brother. He really had no idea of where to look and managed to find trouble wherever he went.

# The Fugitive (September 1963–August 1967)

Dr. Richard Kimble (David Janssen) was an innocent on the lam. Wrongfully convicted of the murder of his wife, he had good reason to never stay in the same place for very long after he escaped from police custody when the train carrying him to the electric chair wrecked somewhere in Indiana. We know that his odyssey to find his wife's killer, the one-armed man, ended at a deserted amusement park on the West Coast.

# Horse-Powered Transport

No show moved more people across TV Land than *Wagon Train*, which starred Ward Bond as wagon-master. Set in the pre–Civil War days, the train of covered Conestoga wagons left Saint Joseph, Missouri, for California on a weekly basis (starting in the fall of 1957). Nine years of continually crossing TV's Heart Land through the Rocky Mountains and on into the Pacific time zone took a toll on this show. Originally a one-hour production, *Wagon Train* took ninety minutes to complete the same run by the time it came to the end of its road in 1968. *Tales of Wells Fargo* (1957–62) was about the legendary and very real company that began as a horse-drawn transport business and developed into a banking empire. Dale Robertson starred as transport agent Jim Hardie. *Stagecoach West* (1960–61) starred Wayne Rogers as Luke Perry—the man holding the reins and taking people and gold shipments from town to town in the Wild West.

# Rail Transport

*Iron Horse* (1966–68) kept Dale Robertson on the move in the role of Ben Calhoun—the owner of the Buffalo & Scalplock Railroad,which was laying track across the American frontier. *Supertrain* (February 1979–July 1979) was a big advance over *Iron Horse* and a much bigger failure, too. Its atomic-powered engine raced from coast to coast in thirty-six hours, pulling cars that contained a disco, gym, and a swimming pool.

# Water Transport

*Riverboat* (1959–61) starred Darren McGavin as the captain of the Enterprise, which cruised the Mississippi River during the 1840s. Burt Reynolds was the boat's pilot—his first regular role on TV. *The Mississippi* (1983–84) was another show about boating down America's premier inland waterway. Ralph Waite (the former woodcutter of Walton's Mountain) starred as a lawyer turned boat captain. The cast included Linda Miller, Jackie Gleason's daughter. The greatest sailing ship in all of TV Land was *The Love Boat* (1977–86). Filmed aboard the *Pacific Princess*, this series starred Gavin MacLeod as Captain Merrill Stubing. Fred Grandy played the role of an assistant purser. Grandy later won real-life election to the United States House of Representatives.

# GOING TO SCHOOL IN TV LAND

The schools of TV Land have always had distinct advantages that ordinary schools can't match. They're easier to get to. They don't last as long. The teachers are nicer. You don't have to turn in your homework with the rest of the class.

If you went to high school in TV Land during the fifties, you probably attended some classes taught by *Our Miss Brooks* (Eve Arden) at Madison High, or by *Mr. Peepers* (Wally Cox) at Jefferson Junior High School. *Mr. Novak* (a.k.a. James Franciscus), who taught at Jefferson High School, in Los Angeles, was the most popular teacher in the sixties.

In *Welcome Back, Kotter*, Gabe Kaplan played the man who taught the barely educable "Sweathogs" of James Buchanan High School, in Brooklyn, New York. *Lucas Tanner* (a.k.a. David Hartman) taught at Harry S. Truman Memorial High School in Webster Groves, Missouri, and rivaled Kotter for the accolade of the best-liked teacher of the seventies.

*Head of the Class*, which starred Howard Hesseman as teacher Charlie Hoover at Millard Fillmore High School in New York, was the set-in-school sitcom of choice in the eighties. By the end of the decade, and continuing into the next, the favorite became *Saved by the Bell*. Set at Bayside High School in Palisades, California (with Dennis Haskins as Principal Belding), this series became phenomenally popular.

While all of these schools are mythical, there are several high schools in the Los Angeles area that have doubled for those of TV Land. They include:

- John Marshall High School—seen on *Mr. Novak*
  Location: 3939 Tracy Street, Los Angeles, California
- Burroughs High School—seen on *The Wonder Years*
  Location: 1920 Clark Avenue, Burbank, California
- Grant High School—seen on *Beverly Hills 90210*
  Location: 13000 Oxnard Street, Studio City, California
- Van Nuys High School—seen on *Life Goes On*
  Location: 6535 Cedros Avenue, Van Nuys, California

**Alumni Notes:**
Ron Howard and Debbie Reynolds both went to Burroughs High School. Robert Redford, Don Drysdale, Natalie Wood, Marilyn Monroe, Paula Abdul, and Jane Russell all went to Van Nuys High School.

## Other Leading High Schools of TV Land

| | |
|---|---|
| Jefferson High | *Happy Days* |
| Orbit High | *The Jetsons* |
| Fillmore High | *Laverne and Shirley* |
| Whitman High | *Room 222* |
| Westwood High | *The Partridge Family* |
| Holmes High | *Cos* |
| Lockspur High | *Isis* |
| West Beverly Hills High | *Beverly Hills 90210* |
| New York City High School of the Performing Arts | *Fame* |

# Getting a Higher Education

***TV Land's Top Five College Students
and the Schools They Went To***
John-Boy Walton (*The Waltons*) went to Boatwright University. Dick Grayson, a.k.a. Robin (*Batman*), was a student at Hudson University. Clark Kent (*Superman*) was a graduate of Metropolis University. Denise Huxtable (*A Different World*) studied at Hillman College. Dobie Gillis attended S. Peter Pryor Junior College.

# CAMPS AND RESORTS OF TV LAND

"The Adventures of Spin and Marty" (presented as part of *The Mickey Mouse Club*) was a serial set at the make-believe Triple R Camp for Boys. Its thirty episodes ran during the winter of 1955. Tim Considine starred as Spin Evans and David Stollery was Marty Markham. "The Further Adventures of Spin and Marty" added thirteen more episodes that also featured Annette Funicello and the girls of the Circle H Camp. They ran in the winter of 1957. "The New Adventures of Spin and Marty" added an additional dozen episodes, which were run in the fall of 1958.

*Guestward Ho!* took its name from the fictional, dilapidated dude ranch in New Mexico around which this series was set. This sitcom was about a New York City couple and their son who abandon urban life for a more laid-back lifestyle in the desert sun. They buy the ranch and discover that life is really no less harried here than it was back East. *Guestward Ho!* starred Mark Miller as Bill Horton, Joanne Dru as his wife, and Flip Mark as their boy, Brook. Dru is the sister of Peter Marshall, the TV game show host. The cast also included J. Carroll Naish (who had once portrayed Charlie Chan on TV) in the role an Indian chief named Hawkeye. The series ran from September of 1960 until September of 1961. *Camp Runamuck* was a sitcom about two summer camps, Runamuck for boys and Divine for girls, located on opposite shores of a lake. It was an uneasy and mostly unfunny coexistence; the series ran only during the 1965–66 TV season.

*Holiday Lodge* was a make-believe resort, located in the Catskill Mountains of New York, which featured the comedy team of Wayne and Schuster as its recreational directors, Johnny Miller and Frank Boone. Running from the end of June 1961 through the first week of the following October, this show was put on as a summer replacement for *The Jack Benny Show*. *Dirty Dancing* was set at the fictitious Kellerman's Mountain Resort, another Catskill Mountains vacation spot. It was based on the 1987 movie of the same title. While the film was a hit, this sitcom was a big loser and ran only briefly from the end of October 1988 until the middle of January of 1989. Patrick Cassidy played the heartthrob dance instructor, Johnny Castle. McLean Stevenson played the resort's owner, Max Kellerman.

# PRO SPORTS IN TV LAND

Though professional sports has long been given near-saturation coverage on television, it hasn't been all that popular an activity within TV Land itself. While the ratings for NFL football are consistently huge, for example, there have been only a couple of series set on gridirons.

*Semi-Tough*, based on the movie (which was based on a Dan Jenkins novel), was a sitcom about the professional New York Bulls. David Hasselhoff (the future *Knight Rider*) starred along with Markie Post and former football pro Bubba Smith. The Bulls began their network run at the end of May, 1980, and were run off the field in less than a month.

*1st & Ten*, the story of the California Bulls pro team, was more successful. It debuted in December of 1984 and ran until 1991. Delta Burke (later to become one of the *Designing Women*) played the team's owner. The cast also included former pro greats John Matuszak and O. J. Simpson.

TV Land has, likewise, fielded only a couple of pro baseball teams. *Ball Four*, based on the book by former New York Yankee pitcher Jim Bouton, was a sitcom about the Washington Americans. Bouton starred in the show, along with former football stand-out Ben Davidson. The series lasted only for a month in the fall of 1976 and was the first show to be axed that season. Harry Chapin wrote and sang its theme song.

*The Bay City Blues* was an hour-long drama about the Bay City Bluebirds, a minor league team in California. They belonged to the fictitious Double A Western League but lasted for only four episodes at the network level in the fall of 1983. Co-created by Steven Bochco (of *Hill Street Blues, L.A. Law, St. Elsewhere, Doogie Howser, M.D.*, and *NYPD Blue* fame), this series featured Patrick Cassidy as a bed-wetting ball player and Sharon Stone as his wife.

Basketball became a TV Land sport in September of 1970, when *The Harlem Globetrotters* began appearing in cartoon form. The show went into reruns in 1978. The *real* Globetrotters had a show of their own, *The Harlem Globetrotters Popcorn Machine*, which was the live-action sort. It ran from 1974 to 1976. Rodney Allen Rippy and Avery Schreiber were the two non-hoopsters in the cast.

# MILITARY TV LAND

The fighting forces of TV Land have been trained, stationed, and (in one case) incarcerated at military installations scattered from North America to the South Pacific, from Asia to Europe. Their ranks include foot soldiers, sailors and marines . . . some dramatic and courageous, some cowardly; mostly, however, comedians. From just after the Civil War until the loss of Vietnam, these men and women have fought (or refrained from fighting) to make the world safe from boredom and to keep TV Land the land of the free and easy cheap laugh.

## Post-Civil War Era

| | | |
|---|---|---|
| Fort Apache | Arizona Territory | *Rin Tin Tin* |
| Fort Courage | Missouri | *F Troop* |

A future moronic fighting man of World War II, the less-than-hostile-looking Tim Conway puts on war paint so as to give the tough guys of *F Troop* a scare they'd never forget. *Courtesy of ABC-TV.*

## World War II Era

| Stalag 13 | Germany | *Hogan's Heroes* |
| Fort Baxter | Roseville, Kansas | *Sergeant Bilko* |
| Camp Fremont | Grove City, California | *Sergeant Bilko* |
| Taratupa Island | South Pacific | *McHale's Navy* |

## Korean War Era

| | South Korea | *M★A★S★H* |

## 1950s–1960s

| Camp Henderson | California | *Gomer Pyle* |
| Camp Grace | Midwest | *Dobie Gillis* |
| Camp Crowder | Joplin, Missouri | *Dick Van Dyke* |

## Vietnam

| China Beach | Viet nam | *China Beach* |

# TV LAND LOCK-UPS

*Parole* was the first TV show to feature a prison setting. This 1958 documentary series was shot on location at penal institutions all across America.

*Mariah* was a short-lived drama that ran for one month in the spring of 1987. It was set at the fictional Mariah State Penitentiary.

*Willow B: Women in Prison* starred Carol Lynley, Sally Kirkland, and Elizabeth Hartman as convicts serving time in Section Willow B of El Camino Institution for Women. This series ran during the 1980 TV season.

*On the Rocks* was a jailhouse sitcom set at Alamesa Minimum Security Prison, where petty thief Hector Fuentes found the laughs in life behind bars. It ran for twenty-two episodes between 1975 and 1976.

*Hogan's Heroes*, perhaps the most improbable sitcom of all times, was set in a Nazi POW camp called Stalag 13. It boasted a steam room and services provided by a barber as well as those of a French chef. The series, starring Bob Crane and Werner Klemperer, ran from 1965 to 1971.

# TV LAND MEDIA

*Name of the Game.* Gene Barry was the big boss in this series about the magazine publishing world. *Courtesy of NBC-TV.*

## Leading Newspapers/Services

| | |
|---|---|
| The Daily Planet | Superman |
| The Los Angeles Tribune | Lou Grant |
| The Clarion | Peyton Place |
| The Los Angeles Sun | My Favorite Martian |
| The New York Herald | The Roaring Twenties |
| Independent News Service | The Night Stalker |

## Leading Publications

| | |
|---|---|
| Manhattanite magazine | My World and Welcome to It |
| People magazine | Name of the Game |
| Crime magazine | Name of the Game |
| Glitter magazine | Glitter |

## Leading TV Stations

| | | |
|---|---|---|
| WJM | Twin Cities, Minnesota | The Mary Tyler Moore Show |
| WYN | Boston, Massachusetts | Goodnight, Beantown |
| WBFC | Buffalo, New York | Buffalo Bill |
| KTNS | Boulder, Colorado | Mork and Mindy |
| WZAZ | Fernwood, Ohio | Fernwood 2-Night |
| KSFB | San Francisco, California | The Smothers Brothers Comedy Hour |

## Leading Radio Stations

| | | |
|---|---|---|
| WKRP | Cincinnati, Ohio | WKRP in Cincinnati |
| KBHR | Cicely, Alaska | Northern Exposure |
| KJCM | San Francisco, California | Midnight Caller |
| WGEO | Washington, D.C. | FM |

# HEALTH SERVICES IN TV LAND

## Recommended Hospitals and Clinics

Blair General Hospital — *Dr. Kildare*
County General Hospital — *Ben Casey*
University Medical Center — *Medical Center*
St. Eligius (a.k.a. St. Elsewhere) — *St. Elsewhere*
Family Practice Center/
   Lang Memorial Hospital — *Marcus Welby, M.D.*
Hope Memorial Hospital — *Chicago Hope*

## Accredited Doctors

*GP's*
Dr. Steven Rossi
Drs. Marcus Welby and Steven Kiley
Dr. Alex Stone

*Surgeons and Specialists*
Dr. Ben Casey (neurosurgery)
Dr. Doogie Howser
Dr. Bones McCoy (space medicine)
Dr. Joe Gannon
Dr. Heathcliffe Huxtable (OB/GYN)

*Shrinks*
Dr. Bob Hartley

Dr. Joyce Brothers
Dr. Frasier Crane

*Sex Expert*
Dr. Ruth Westheimer

*Frontier Doctors*
Dr. Michaela Quinn
Dr. Galen Adams
Dr. Joel Fleischman

*Dentists*
Dr. Jerry Helper
Dr. Jerry Robinson

*Coroner*
Dr. R. Quincy

The good doctor Marcus Welby, played by Robert Young who was the father who knew best, was the focus of this medical series. It was set in Santa Monica, California, but its producers used the Santa Barbara County Courthouse for the show's exterior shot. *Courtesy of ABC-TV.*

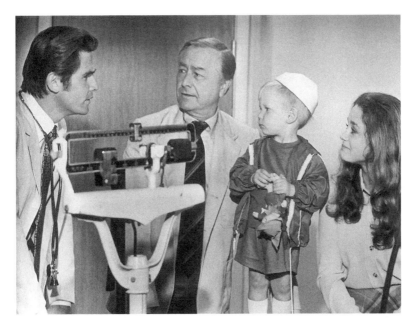

# SOAPVILLE

There are towns throughout the land that know no moral peace, in which tragedies never end, where tears never dry, philandering goes uninterrupted, and mayhem occurs either right on the scene or excruciatingly nearby. These are the towns and cities of Soapville—some actual places, others created in nightmares and covered by the cosmetology of TV drama.

| | |
|---|---|
| *As the World Turns* | Oakdale (Midwest) |
| *All My Children* | Pine Valley, New York |
| *Another World* | Bay City |
| *General Hospital* | Port Charles |
| *Edge of Night* | Monticello |
| *Guiding Light* | Springfield |
| *Love of Life* | Barrowsville, Rose Hill |
| *Loving* | Corinth |
| *One Life to Live* | Llanview |
| *Rituals* | Wingfield, Virginia |
| *Search for Tomorrow* | Henderson |
| *Secret Storm* | Woodbridge |
| *Secrets of Midland Heights* | Midwest |
| *The Young and the Restless* | Genoa City |

# PARANORMAL LIFE

## Ghosts

The Show: *Topper*
The Paranormals: Neil (a St. Bernard dog) George and Marion
  Kirby

The Show: *The Ghost and Mrs. Muir*
The Paranormal: Captain Daniel Gregg (a nineteenth-century
  mariner)

The Show: *Casper,*
  *The Friendly Ghost*
The Paranormal:
  Casper
  (a dead child)

A ghost of a St. Bernard
named Neil materializes
and gets taken for a ride
by Topper.
*Courtesy of Mediacast.*

# Possessed People

The Show: *Bewitched*
The Possessed: Samantha, Serena, Endora, Maurice, Aunt Clara, Uncle Arthur, Esmerelda, Dr. Bombay, Tabitha

# Angels

The Show: *The Smothers Brothers Show*
The Angel: Tommy Smothers as an apprentice angel

The Show: *Good Heavens*
The Angel: Carl Reiner as an angel in a business suit

The Show: *Highway to Heaven*
The Angel: Michael Landon as a probationary angel

# Enchanted Humans

Jeannie—*I Dream of Jeannie*
Mr. Roarke—*Fantasy Island*

# INDELIBLE IMAGERY DENOTING TV LAND

Just as the golden glow emanating from the yellow brick road signals the approach to Oz, so too are there signs and symbols that let people know that they're about to enter TV Land.

## The Twilight Zone

The sight of an infinity symbol—an elongated, flattened figure eight—appearing in a star-bright night sky is the visual tip-off that the viewer is about to enter *The Twilight Zone*.

## Ben Casey

It didn't take a brain surgeon to know a brain surgeon when the latter was a hairy-chested fellow known as Ben Casey. *Ben Casey*, which starred Vince Edwards, had one of the most distinctive openings in TV history. Viewers knew that they were about to meet the good doctor, as he made his appointed rounds in County General Hospital, just as soon as a series of symbols depicting Man, Woman, Birth, Death, and Infinity flashed on the screen at the start of each show. This infinity sign wasn't the same one used by *The Twilight Zone*; Casey favored the three-dot ellipsis version.

# Checkmate

The mesmerizing image of a melting chessboard, with its black-and-white squares liquefying and spilling into one another, signaled the start of each episode of *Checkmate*. This early 1960s series (which starred Sebastian Cabot and Doug McLure) was about a high-priced San Francisco detective agency.

# Zorro

The letter *Z* is one of TV Land's all-time icons. Whenever this last letter of the alphabet filled the screen all by itself, viewers could be sure they had tuned into the series that depicted the adventures of a daring aristocrat named Don Diego de la Vega. A champion of the common man, Don Diego can be likened to fellow TV Land aristocrat Bruce Wayne. Like Bruce (a.k.a. *Batman*), Don Diego assumed a secret identity and wore a black mask and cape whenever he battled bad guys. He was, of course, the "bold renegade [who] carves a *Z* with his blade/a *Z* that stands for *Zorro*."

Guy Williams, the man behind the mask, carried a sharp sword which made his mark (a Z, of course) all around the Monterey, California, area; at least he did back when the Golden State was still a Spanish colony and home to people so oblivious that a man wearing such an obvious outfit could go undetected night after night. *Courtesy of ABC-TV.*

# TV LAND TOURIST SERVICES

## Spending the Night

| | | |
|---|---|---|
| Barclay Hotel | New York City | *The Ann Sothern Show* |
| Salish Lodge | Twin Peaks | *Twin Peaks* |
| Shady Rest Inn | Hooterville | *Petticoat Junction* |
| Hotel Carlton | San Francisco | *Have Gun, Will Travel* |
| St. Gregory Hotel | San Francisco | *Hotel* |
| Stafford Inn | Vermont | *Newhart* |

## Food & Drink

| | | |
|---|---|---|
| Snappy Lunch Cafe | Mayberry | *The Andy Griffith Show* |
| Cheers Bar | Boston | *Cheers* |
| Archie's Place | Queens | *Archie's Place* |
| Frank's Place | New Orleans | *Frank's Place* |
| Mel's Diner | Phoenix | *Alice* |
| Arnold's Drive-In | Milwaukee | *Happy Days* |
| New York Deli | Boulder | *Mork and Mindy* |
| Dino's | Los Angeles | *77 Sunset Strip* |
| Long Branch Saloon | Dodge City | *Gunsmoke* |
| Delmonico's | Dodge City | *Gunsmoke* |

# TV LAND
## Live Entertainment

| | | |
|---|---|---|
| Copacabana | New York City | *The Danny Thomas Show* |
| Tropicana | New York City | *I Love Lucy* |
| Shell Bar, Hawaiian Village Hotel | Honolulu | *Hawaiian Eye* |

# AFTERWORD

# TV Land Doomsday Scenario

It begins with a Wal-Mart being built atop Walton's Mountain. Then Fred Flintstone's old stomping grounds get dug up and transformed into a toxic waste containment center. Next, the Ponderosa Ranch is shorn of its pines and carved up into tracts of time-share vacation condos. Soon after that, Metropolis is ravaged by gangs brandishing submachine guns firing Krypton bullets, precluding any rescue attempt that Superman might otherwise make.

Of course, all this sounds even father-out than far-fetched, but there is no denying that TV Land (as we now know it) will be increasingly vulnerable to the physically destructive forces of what land developers euphemistically call "progress." Unlike battlefields, the birthplaces of presidents, monuments such as the Statue of Liberty and the Liberty Bell, or stretches of wilderness that harbor an endangered species or two, no part of TV Land, with only a handful of exceptions, is ever likely to be designated as a park, historical site, landmark, or refuge preserved and protected by the power of law.

Consistent with the paradox that is TV Land, its future (despite the inevitability of loss) also portends some significant gain. With each passing TV season comes new shows set in new locations . . . assuring that the width and breadth of TV Land will expand. Because of the current profusion and proliferation of new networks, cable stations, and satellite delivery systems, we're likely to keep seeing many of the old familiar places for years to come. Huge blocks of programming will likely be filled by shows already considered to be classics as well as those contemporary series that are on their way to becoming tomorrow's vintage fare.

In short, the Cheers bar may one day become a soup kitchen but—as seen on TV—it will remain the place, frozen in time via videotape, where you can go and hear echoes of the song claiming that "you want a place where everybody knows your name."